Bridging the Circle

Transition through Quality Circle Time

Lesson plans for years 6 & 7

Anne Cowling and Penny Vine

Positive Press

First published 2001 by Positive Press Ltd
28A Gloucester Road
Trowbridge
Wiltshire
BA14 0AA
England

Reprinted 2003

Text © Anne Cowling and Penny Vine, 2001
Revised version of a handbook originally produced
for internal training purposes by Leeds Training and Enterprise
Council in conjunction with Leeds City Council

ISBN 0 9530122 2 0

Printed in England

Contents

Bridging the Circle and its development through the 'I, Too' Partnership

Well daughter, I'll tell you
Life for you won't be easy
Climbing those school stairs will be pitiless and hard

But you must climb on dizzily
Right to the top
Even though some may say
"Now's the time to STOP"

Kyle Thomas
Quarry Mount Primary School, Leeds

Above is an extract from *Dad's Life and Advice*, a poem by a primary school pupil in inner city Leeds. This poem and others were inspired by the work of Langston Hughes, a Black American poet writing during the Harlem Renaissance in the 1930s.

The 'I, Too' Project takes its name from Langston Hughes' poem *I, Too*, which confers ideas of being included and taking a rightful place in society. The Leeds Training and Enterprise Council (Leeds TEC) and other key local partners under the umbrella of the 'I, Too' Partnership began work in 1997 with Leeds inner city communities to promote social inclusion.

The TEC formulated a successful bid for Single Regeneration Budget funding; it also supports the partnership with additional funding from its reserves and from TEC discretionary funding. 'I, Too' is a flagship initiative which demonstrates recorded good practice and is part of Leeds TEC's legacy to the City of Leeds, providing a unique insight into tackling regeneration through learning and skills.

The 'I, Too' partnership promotes inclusion in a variety of ways. Projects were developed using National Open College Accreditation to raise educational attainment; work was also developed around supporting young people in danger of exclusion from school. As part of this work, teachers, parents and pupils alike communicated the need for more help and support around transition from primary to high school.

In 1999, the Fresh Start initiative of 'I, Too' gained success in bringing schools and parents together to support children who had not coped with the transition from primary to high school. Anne Cowling, an innovative PSHE co-ordinator at Agnes Stewart High School in Leeds came to the partnership with an idea for developing Circle work on the subject of transition.

'I, Too' supported developmental work with both key stage 2 and 3 pupils and parents. The issues discussed at these sessions plus other work with young people through the Project contributed to Anne's concept of 'Bridging the Circle' which she co-wrote with colleague Penny Vine.

The resulting resource must therefore be credited in part to the young people of inner city Leeds, particularly Agnes Stewart C of E High School and St Peters Primary School.

Claire Whiteley
I, Too Project Manager

Foreword

"Education must enable all pupils to respond positively to the opportunities and challenges in which we live and work . . ."

- QCA *The review of the National Curriculum in England: Consultation materials '99.*

One of the key experiences of change for pupils is to move from the smaller, familiar warm world of the primary school to the chillier, seemingly impersonal world of the secondary school. There is no doubt this transition can prove to be a very anxious experience. Children have real fears around the 'initation' myths and truths of their local secondary school. Self-esteem can plummet and emotions soar.

Schools need to explore as many ways as possible to equip young people to meet the challenges of this move. Powerlessness and fear are huge inhibitors and many children fail as a result to reach their full academic, social, personal, moral, cultural or spiritual potential. The last ten years in primary schools have seen a groundswell of interest in the development of circle time. The actual practice may well be patchy, nevertheless many primary teachers are struggling, through the structures of circle time, to improve self-esteem, social skills, emotional literacy, a sense of citizenship and a feeling of being part of a team. In other words circle time, if run by a knowledgeable and skilled teacher, has the potential to meet the new 2000 agenda for education. However, up till now, this positive weekly experience in primary schools abruptly stops at the age of eleven. The real potential of this approach to help children build a bridge of understanding and confidence to move from the primary into the secondary world has only been explored by a small number of schools and local authorities. Help is at hand!

It is with a sigh of relief and huge pleasure that I can recommend this book by Anne and Penny. It has an enormous contribution to make to education. Through their own sensitive thoughtful research and their ability to work collaboratively and enthusiastically with Leeds teachers, they have created a series of lesson plans that can be immediately implemented. These lesson plans however are richer than merely a collection of 'do-able' ideas. Anne and Penny have given great attention to the aims, process, rationale and more importantly, the outcomes. Teachers can be confident of the knowledge, skills and values that they are helping the pupils to explore. In addition, they offer a selection of back up written work to support the emotional work facilitated by the circle lesson. Schools can be confident that they are working within the spirit of the new government initiatives and guidelines relating to PSHE and Citizenship.

I cannot recommend this book highly enough. It is vital that children perceive their educational experience to be a continuum of personal and social growth. This series of lesson plans will help them move confidently, responsibly and courageously from the primary to the secondary experience. Anne Cowling and Penny Vine deserve real congratulations for supporting children and teachers during this vital time. It is a contribution of 'excellence'.

Jenny Mosley

Acknowledgements

The authors: Anne Cowling and Penny Vine are teacher advisers for PSHCE for the Leeds City Council LEA.

Without the support of the 'I, Too' Partnership and Leeds TEC, particularly the perceptiveness of Ruth Cockcroft, this project would not have got off the ground. Grateful thanks to Adam Ranson and Trish Sandbach at the Leeds Development Education Centre for their thoughts and contributions, both Cathy DePledge of Ebor Gardens Primary School and Theresa Walker of Shakespeare Primary School for piloting the material with their classes, and to all the year 6 students from these two schools who took part and spoke so openly about their feelings. Thanks also to teachers Heather Hobbs and Liz Alcock at Agnes Stewart C/E High School and to all the year 7 students who have taken part in piloting these lesson plans. Thanks to parents and students of the Fresh Start Inclusion programme whose thoughts have been invaluable, and to Felicity Cowling and Naomi Williams and their friends and parents who have contributed some very useful and personal insights in the year of their transition to secondary schools. Thank you also to Simon for help with proof reading.

Our particular grateful thanks go to Jenny Mosley whose Quality Circle Time model directly influenced the structure of our lesson plans. The model is discussed in more detail in the Introduction, and her publications are mentioned in the bibliography and resources sections. We hope to enjoy her continuing interest and support in our work.

Finally, thank you to Trisha Firth and her young students at Bankside Primary School and Zoe Pearson with the students of 7LMC at Agnes Stewart for allowing us to photograph their circle time session.

Project supported by:

LEEDS
CITY COUNCIL

Training and
Enterprise
Council

Circle Time for Transition from Primary to Secondary Schools

The aim of this publication is to provide practical teaching resources for both year 6 and year 7 teachers who want to tackle issues around the transition from primary to secondary school in PSHE/Citizenship or form tutor lessons. For primary school teachers there are six lesson plans which look at the fears and concerns around being bullied, not managing work, getting lost, missing friends and other issues. For secondary school teachers there are two lesson plans which have 'taster' or 'open' days in mind - one for students, and one for parents.

Following this are six lesson plans for the PSHE/form tutor which look at adapting to change and acclimatising self in relation to the new establishment, knowing how, when and where to get help, looking at changes in expectations, dealing with loss, and changes in friendships.

Transition

I'm mainly worried about being bullied - Charlotte age 11

The transition period can be a very testing and emotional time, as young people move from a thoroughly familiar and stable situation to a situation which is neither. At primary school they may have responsibilities and status, established and positive relationships with friends, teachers, supervisors and administration staff. Many young people will have spent seven years in the same place and will have a rooted sense of self in relation to the establishment. They move from this to a situation of uncertainty, new relationships, new rules and expectations, and very little sense of self as part of the establishment. It is a big jump, with underlying fears and anxieties and apprehensions providing a possible backdrop to all performance - whether social, or academic. This is true for all children, just as it would be for an adult starting a new job. On top of all of this, the emotional and cognitive adjustments to body changes due to puberty are to be taken into account. Relationships with teachers take much longer to build at secondary school, with a new teacher for each subject, which in turn places more emphasis and perhaps more strain on peer relationships. The general ethos of the school and peer attitudes towards school, teachers and school work may determine positive or negative patterns of behaviour - concerns about peer expectations are intense for young people of this age.

Most of my friends behave worse at secondary. - Lucy age 12

This transition 'cocktail' provides many opportunities for things to go wrong. It is likely that, for those who are prone to anxiety, the transition might bring about a surplus of reflex 'coping' responses to potentially threatening situations.

So those who have shown chaotic/reclusive/antisocial behaviour in the past may well display these patterns to extremes during this time of uncertainty. Many of today's young people have their own experiences of family transitions that may have been difficult - break up of families and acquiring new step families.

To these young people, change may be painfully threatening. Fear and anxiety can preoccupy our minds to the extent that we cannot learn and think clearly and perform to the best of our ability. The prevailing conditions which need to be present for effective learning to take place involve feeling accepted, secure and having self-esteem.

It is easy to understand how work and behaviour can suffer and spiral dangerously downwards at the point of transition.

I hadn't realised that I would be so tired at the end of the day to start with - Nazir age 12

Many schools make attempts to ease the process of transition in some way - such as providing a year 7 base where the students have the stability of a permanent classroom and a smaller number of teachers, primary-secondary liaison on learning progression from key stage two to three, support services or peer counselling/mentoring systems, all of which are helpful. Above all, **preparation** for any kind of transition helps, as does talking it through before, during and after. These lesson plans attempt to help young people to think ahead, prepare themselves for change, and to acknowledge their feelings about the change, before, during and after. If we are prepared and aware, we are more able to control ourselves in ways that are helpful and not destructive. If we do get caught off guard and lose control over a situation, it helps to talk about it, to review and to plan for similar situations. The circle time lesson plans aim to provide the opportunities to do these things: the planning, the doing, the reviewing, whilst at the same time always building and reinforcing positive regard towards self and others. They attempt to deal with issues which most young people worry about when moving on to secondary, namely bullying, getting lost in the big school, work being too difficult and losing friends,[1] as well as issues that perhaps they haven't yet thought about, such as changes in routines at home.

The single session for parents/carers and children aims to give an insight into the practical and emotional issues which will arise for all the family. This is in recognition of the fact that moving on to secondary school affects not only the child but the family as well, and of how mutual consideration and support at this crucial time is advantageous for all concerned.

Home life definitely changed once she started at secondary. Everything was much more rushed on a morning . . . and the bag packing! I reckon she must have a PhD in it now, but it was murder at first. We eventually got into a routine of checking the bag the night before - Janet (a mum)

---

1 See Tattum, D. and Herbert, G. (1993) *Countering Bullying: Initiatives by Schools and Local Authorities* Theme three - Transition, and Edinburgh Family Service Unit's *Primary/Secondary Transition Programme*

Circle time

Circle time is showing signs of becoming the rule rather than the exception in primary schools. Secondary schools are just beginning to see the value of this person-centred teaching model. The lessons in this book use the approach as advocated by Jenny Mosley, which is developed, structured and thoughtful, and has the needs of the learning child firmly at the centre of its pedagogy.

Circle time is a process-based approach to learning which aims to enhance emotional well-being, encouraging self-awareness, empathy and positive communication. There are many positive reasons for following the Jenny Mosley model of 'Quality Circle Time'.[2] Jenny Mosley believes in a whole school approach to circle time: her ideal is a school 'in which every child and adult belongs to a programme of timetabled Circle Time meetings',[3] and she sees circle time as a forum for individual and organisational change. Her recent publication on circle time for secondary schools[4] contains ten lesson plans or 'circle scripts' as well as other rounds, games and quizzes which would provide excellent resources for dovetailing into, or following on from, these resources for transition.

Circle time takes PSHE into the wider curriculum and even into the wider community because of the personal qualities and skills which it encourages. Engaging both mind and body through theme-linked games, rounds, silent statements, and open forums, the lesson format develops trust and security within a group, aims to raise emotional literacy and self-esteem, enhance personal responsibility and improve the quality of relationships. It encourages appropriate self-disclosure, co-operation, listening skills, intra-personal and inter-personal skills. It uses positive assertive language and can tackle all PSHE issues successfully, e.g. friendship, bullying, sexual harassment, racism, stress, nutrition, body changes and drugs. It encourages all pupils to speak confidently and to listen, to feel that their contribution has value, to engage in problem-solving to help each other, to be open, and to create a non-hostile environment for all. Circle time can also be used on behaviour modification programmes with a great deal of success. Students with behavioural needs often appreciate the pace and security gained from the structure of the lesson. It is possible to cover and receive awards for certain key skills[5] which can be a great incentive and reward for all students, but particularly for those who see 'academic work' as unwinnable.

The circle format

Everybody, including teachers and assistants, is to sit on chairs in a circle. If a flipchart is necessary, it helps to have that as part of the circle too. It is possible to run circle time with large or small groups, and with all age groups.

---

2   See Mosley, J. (1993) *Turn Your School Round*, and Mosley, J. (1996) *Quality Circle Time in the Primary Classroom*
3   Mosley, J. (1996) *Quality Circle Time in the Primary Classroom* p.6
4   Mosley, J. and Tew, M. (1999) *Quality Circle Time in the Secondary School - A handbook of good practice,* David Fulton Publishers Ltd
5   Key Skills in communication (speaking and listening), working with others etc. National Open College Network (NOCN)

The structure

Each lesson takes approximately 45 minutes. If the logsheets in appendix 3 are filled in by students at the end of each lesson, it will take an hour. Each lesson plan has seven sections:

- Ground rules
- Game
- Round
- Silent Statement
- Open Forum
- Game
- Round

Rules - see appendix 1

It helps if . . .

- the rules are adhered to strictly - eg. put-downs and talking out of turn are noticed and dealt with, so that the level of trust and security is maintained. The 'no names' rule helps to maintain trust and openness. For example, aunty Peggy would probably prefer everybody in her nephew's class not to know she's having problems with her periods! 'Somebody' or 'someone I know' would be the alternative.

Games

It helps . . .

- not to underestimate their value. We have tried to make the games thematic and co-operative, where nobody feels to have 'lost' or is excluded. Teachers may feel unsure about the use of games to begin with, but if they persist they should find that co-operative games promote positive relationships, good feeling and create a feeling of togetherness and community. They involve the use of many skills - working together, co-operating, listening without interruption, speaking, good eye contact, and allowing others to take their turn. Where there is co-operation, good feeling is generated, which is the right atmosphere for learning. They help build up a positive and warm emotional climate and break down tension and inhibitions through laughter. Try asking questions about what happened in the game: how people responded, whether anything seemed unfair, what did people notice? Moral values can be reinforced through such cognitive discussions and reflections.

6

Rounds

Each person in the circle in turn completes a sentence or makes some sort of statement.

It helps if . . .

- an object is passed around (e.g. a stone or shell) for the rounds, which clarifies whose turn it is to speak. The object does tend to develop a symbolic significance for the class, so it helps to use the same one each time;
- people are allowed to say pass, but if two people say pass, the tutor gives the next person a thinking moment - a turn to speak comes more quickly when the person before you says pass and it's often tempting to say   pass rather than make a contribution. If everyone starts to say pass, it may be that the class need more time to think - ask them to prepare their statements in pairs;
- sensitivity is shown to students who do not find it easy to speak out in a large group. Private encouragement outside the group for progress made would be appropriate;
- the tutor briefly thanks each person in turn (with good eye contact!), and if a statement is not loud enough for others to hear, to repeat it so others can hear it;
- laughing at what people say is discouraged unless a laugh is really intended. People who get pigeon-holed as comedians must be allowed to be serious.

Pairwork

Sometimes a round can be prepared in pairs.

It helps if . . .

- partners stay in the circle and incline themselves towards each other;
- good listening body language and eye contact are encouraged;
- students are encouraged to work with a variety of people and genders.

Silent Statements

Students are invited to stand up and cross the circle if they agree with a statement. This allows people to vote with their feet, and is a very powerful tool for allowing expression about issues which may be difficult to voice, and for gaining depth of awareness.

It helps if . . .

- the statements are read out fairly rapidly;

- students are encouraged/praised for being honest with the more difficult statements;
- the teacher is aware when group members tire of this. Provide alternatives like raise your hand, or just stand up.

Open Forum

This provides a space in the lesson for real life situations to be brought into the circle, giving an opportunity for the students to develop their human problem-solving skills and to offer help. Initially, the teacher could present the scenario by role-playing the character. Alternatively, a class member could have prepared the scenario in advance. Eventually, the forum should feel to be a safe enough environment to which people will want to bring their own problems. Through listening to the thoughts and feelings of others, students are able to develop empathy, and to make helpful suggestions which may even involve a personal commitment - a model of good citizenship. For teachers who wish to promote peer counselling skills, the skills of listening and helping could be taken a stage further by encouraging the students to 'reflect' back or summarise the situation before they make suggestions, in the way that a counsellor would.

It helps if . . .
- the speaker mentions no names - 'somebody' is a good alternative (this is one of the rules - but it may need to be reiterated at this point);
- people raise their hands if they wish to offer help;
- the correct language is encouraged on every occasion. The tutor may need to prompt: 'would it help if I/you/we';
- every offer of help is graciously received, and thanked;
- the recipient of the help clarifies whether the help offered will or will not be useful and why;
- the recipient summarises a course of action after all help has been gratefully received;

- students can bring up issues which may involve other class members, and which in a spirit of openness can often be safely sorted out because no names are mentioned, and because no blame is attached. Exercise caution, however, and be aware of people knowing who the 'somebody' is. Emotions can get out of hand. In situations like this it is easier to deal with the situation outside of the public arena. It can be a good idea to explain that this is a forum where they can bring their problems but it might bethat some problems are too personal and could be brought to the teacher instead.

Closing round

It helps if . . .

- the tutor does this in preference to the end game if there are time limitations. It is an important reinforcement and 'logging off' activity which encourages pupils to reflect on, summarise and celebrate what they have learnt during the lesson, and to disengage their minds from serious matters.

Emotional and multiple intelligences

Circle time is a learning vehicle which provides the mixed brain diet recommended by proponents of 'Accelerated Learning' and 'Emotional Intelligence'.[6] Alistair Smith remarks on how teachers tend to teach within their own 'comfort zone', which may not be the same comfort zone as that of their pupils, and that much of teaching today is in direct conflict with what we now know about the brain. Not only do we now know that people have different learning preferences - auditory, visual or kinaesthetic; we also know that our emotional needs affect our learning on a very basic biological level. In order to learn effectively, we need to feel we belong, to feel safe (emotionally and physically), to have a well defined sense of self, and to have enough positive feedback to maintain our self-esteem and self-belief. Reading around these areas of accelerated learning and emotional intelligence is highly recommended.

Practical questions/comments associated with introducing circle time

How do we organise classroom furniture?

Secondary school furniture in particular is not conducive to PSHE lessons, with desks being the perfect barriers to openness and democracy. The ideal would be a large classroom with a carpet and enough tables to seat everybody in groups of four or five and room for drama work when there is a need. Where possible, appoint monitors to organise the classroom before the class arrives so that the lesson can begin with a calm atmosphere. The health and safety implications of students moving furniture are in question here, but classes can move furniture back safely and in silence and it's possible to make it fun - e.g. today there are two rules about moving the furniture - 1) We must be silent - we are only allowed to make sign language to each other, and 2) No furniture must make any noise.

I don't feel comfortable with the format

It takes time for teachers to get used to the format and develop their own personal style. Keeping it 'pacey' is vital, and using positive, assertive methods of discipline is equally vital, sticking to the rules of circle time. Also, having fun is part of the whole aim of circle time, to break tension and to build up a positive warm climate. It helps if teachers are interested! Some groups may need a flexible approach to the format, with more emphasis on the games so that group warmth and trust is built up.

6   Smith, Alistair (1996) *Accelerated Learning in the Classroom*
    Gardner, H. (1993) *Multiple Intelligence*
    Goleman, D. (1996) *Emotional Intelligence - Why it matters more than IQ*

Can circle time be damaging if tackled incorrectly?

The value of circle time can be debased if it is not used with focus, sensitivity and progression. It ought to be theme-based and progressive - within the lesson, from lesson to lesson and module to module. The skills which have been learnt must be built upon. Also, if we expect students to develop a high level of emotional literacy, the teachers involved should have a good level of self-awareness and emotional literacy before they start - a lot of emotional damage can be done to students by teachers who do not concern themselves with how their own behaviour affects people! Again, positive, assertive methods of discipline are very helpful.

General points about circle time

It helps if . . .

- tutors take part in all activities;
- tutors use positive language all the time. Language  should be congruent - students know when it is not meant! Students will follow the tutors' lead with developing skills to create a 'no put-down zone'. A positive climate will blossom where the frequent and consistent use of the words, 'thankyou', 'well done', 'that's good', 'excellent' etc. are used. Each individual contribution should be acknowledged in this way.

 Remember that many students will have experienced a rush of adrenalin when it's been their turn to speak, and will need all the encouragement they can get;

- tutors praise students who speak clearly, to encourage confident speaking;
- tutors are safely and maturely open with the students. Silent statements are good for this. Role modelling is important - tutors can be open about trying to deal with their own imperfections;
- a calm assertive and positive approach to discipline is used in the circle;
- tutors stick to the rules themselves;
- you can have fun moments as well as serious moments.

Outcomes and credits

Using circle work, students can develop speaking and listening skills to a sophisticated level. A credit-based national qualification by NOCN includes speaking and listening as one of their key skills, which is worth one credit.[7]

---

7 National Open College Network, see Bibliography

Evidencing and assessment

Evidencing and assessing circle work can be done in several ways:

- using a camcorder to record individual contributions (parental consent may need to be sought);
- using an evaluation sheet for tutor use - see example in appendix 2;
- using a self-assessment sheet - see pupil logs in appendix 3, alternatively, a questionnaire at the end of a module;
- linking the circle time work with the attainment of a key skill with focused outcomes can be useful.

Lesson plan layout

The lesson plans are formatted and laid out in a detailed way in terms of outcomes. Outcomes are outlined in terms of knowledge, awareness, skills and values. The detail allows those who are new to circle time to be clear about why any one activity should happen, and to highlight the complexity of knowledge, skills and values which are covered. We, the authors, had great fun racking our brains over these outcomes, as it ensured that we had to justify the validity of each and every exercise. Needless to say, the average class teacher does not have the time to be thinking about such detail when making up their own circle time sessions, but the learning for us from this labour-intensive approach was that quality lessons occur when they are theme-based, that it helps if all activities relate to the theme and that learning about the theme takes place with each activity - even the games. A subject/issue can be 'plumbed' to ever greater depths throughout the course of a lesson. We particularly see this happening through the course of the silent statements, where the students are asked to comment silently on continually deepening statements. If the open forum/scenario which follows then takes off from that level of depth, intra-personal learning can be fairly intense.

Student logs

The student logs in appendix 3 present an approach to self-evidencing and self-assessing learning and performance. They are structured so that they encourage further intra-personal learning. It may be possible for these to be partly filled in as peer assessment sheets. The 'warm signals' referred to will need to be explained to the students. A warm signal can be a kind comment, a smile, listening well etc. And understanding warm signals is about recognising that people can not only make us feel good about ourselves, but that we too can make others feel good about themselves.

Child protection

To prevent inappropriate public disclosure, it is important that young people know that what they reveal in the circle must feel safe and comfortable for them. They need to know that they can talk to you privately and in confidence if something is worrying them, but they also need to know that if what they say concerns you, you may have to talk to another person about it. Child protection issues often arise in the teaching of PSHE. School child protection officers will be able to help you if you are unsure about anything.

Using the Lesson Plans

Each lesson occupies a double page spread with the book turned sideways, and can be laid open in front of the teacher using it.

See pages 6-9 for discussion and explanation of the structure.

Key to the Lesson Plans

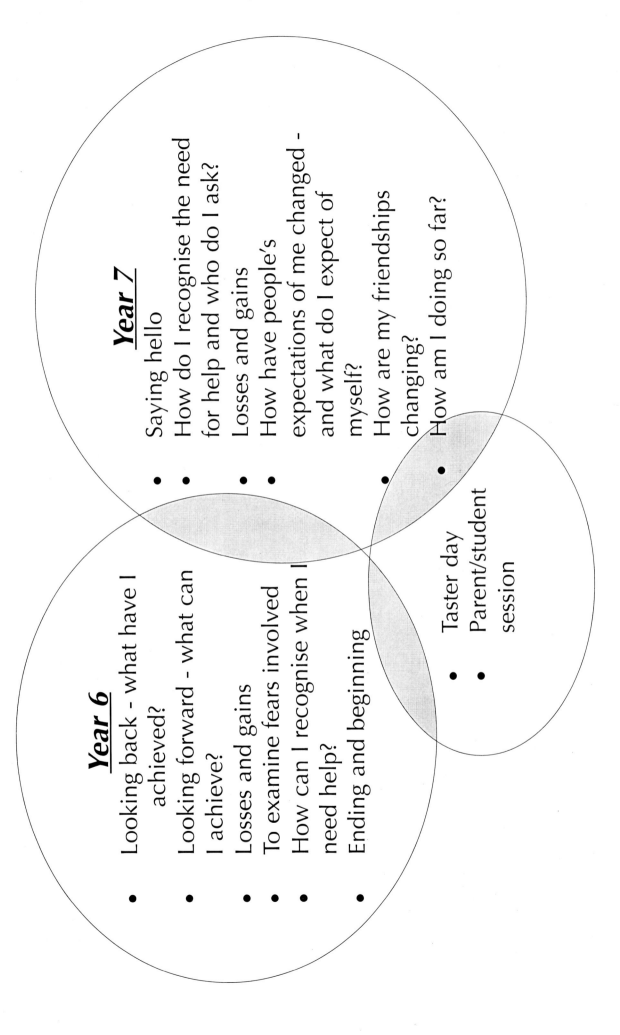

Year 7

- Saying hello
- How do I recognise the need for help and who do I ask?
- Losses and gains
- How have people's expectations of me changed - and what do I expect of myself?
- How are my friendships changing?
- How am I doing so far?

- Taster day
- Parent/student session

Year 6

- Looking back - what have I achieved?
- Looking forward - what can I achieve?
- Losses and gains
- To examine fears involved
- How can I recognise when I need help?
- Ending and beginning

13

Overview of Transition Lesson Plans – Primary

AIM: To assist young people in the process of transition from primary to secondary school	
Lesson	**Details**
1. Looking back – what have I achieved?	To help the students to reflect on all the different things they have achieved at primary school and to become aware of their strengths.
2. Looking forward – what can I achieve?	To help the students to become more aware of the range of positive opportunities and experiences that lie in front of them.
3. Losses and gains	To encourage students to think about the losses and gains associated with change, and to think of ways of managing the losses.
4. To examine in more detail some of the fears involved	To help the students to become aware of dealing with the unknown, recognising that they might not be on their own with their experiences. This is a problem-solving, empowering exercise encouraging positive attitudes, self-awareness and setting of goals.
5. How can I recognise when I need help?	To help with recognising feelings and acting in ways that are constructive.
6. Ending and beginning	To create a positive and prepared feeling about moving on whilst acknowledging apprehensive feelings. Ritualised ending.

Overview of Transition Lesson Plans – Secondary

AIM: To assist young people in the process of transition from primary to secondary school	
Lesson	**Details**
Taster Day	Coming to terms with all that is new – a taste of life in secondary school – getting to know each other.
Taster Day Parent/Student session	Parent–student two-way empathy through transition. Making the adjustments.
1. Saying hello	Openings, establishing safety, security, introducing me – who am I? Relationships, ground rules, getting to know each other. Raising self-esteem and confidence.
2. How do I recognise the need for help and how do I ask for it?	Am I OK? Assertiveness, it's OK to make mistakes, what kind of help do I need and who do I go to?
3. Losses and gains	Helping with the emotions around loss, and offsetting this with the positive aspects of newness.
4. How have people's expectations of me changed and what do I expect of myself?	Ways of dealing with and avoiding the stress and confusion of peer/parent/teacher expectation.
5. How are my friendships changing?	How are we with old and new friends, and how are they with us – win/win approaches.
6. How am I doing so far?	Celebration – how do I get on in the circle, how have I got on in school so far?

Primary Transition Lesson 1

In the week leading up to circle time, the children could be asked to record different kinds of achievements. They could categorise personal, social, physical, academic. Include: sharing, co-operation, taking turns, listening.

AIM: To look back – what have I achieved? To develop self-awareness, positive self-esteem and confidence

Process	Resources	Rationale	Knowledge/Skills/Attitude
1. Introduction and Rules Teacher to explain to the students that the following lessons are to help them all with moving on to secondary school and that today's and next week's lessons are going to be about looking back at how far they have come and at all the things they have achieved so that they can feel confident and good about themselves. Teacher to point out that self-esteem is important to our well-being, particularly during a period of change. Teacher to introduce rules.	*On the flipchart:* 'Moving on to secondary school' 'Looking Back – what have I achieved?' Rules (see Appendix 1).	To help the students understand the overall aim of these lessons and to understand the importance of self-awareness, positive self-esteem and confidence in the process of change.	*I know* what makes me feel good about myself. *I can reflect* on strengths and achievements. *I value* my own achievements.
2. Game Begin by asking the children to reflect on all their different achievements. The game starts by the the whole class making two claps. Then the first person mentions any one achievement. The class then claps twice again and the second person mentions an achievement and so the game goes on. If a child cannot think of a word they can just say achievement.		We want the students to become aware of all the different things they have achieved.	*I know/understand* the meaning of achievement. *I can identify* an achievement of my own.
3. Round Ask children to close their eyes and remember the most important thing that they have learned. Deepen their responses by asking; I wonder what learning you value most at this time in your life? Can you imagine your life without this piece of learning? (Teacher inputs his/her feelings.) Something I have learnt which I really value is ...	*On the flipchart:* 'What do we value most in learning?' 'Something I have learnt which I really value is ...'	To help the students understand what they most value learning in their lives.	*I know/understand* that we need to learn. *I can identify* something I have learnt that I value. *I respect and value* education.

Process	Resources	Rationale	Knowledge/Skills/Attitude
4. Silent Statements Stand up and cross the circle if ... you remember learning to tie your shoe laces; you remember learning how to make friends; you remember hurting someone and learning how to say sorry; you remember lying about something and having to learn about being honest; you remember finding something difficult to learn.		To help students to realise some of the different and important things they have learnt.	As for no. 5
5. Open Forum The teacher reads a letter from a child who has no memories of positive achievement. *Dear Friends,* *Our teacher has asked us to write about the things that we have achieved. Well I can't even spell, and I certainly can't do my maths. I wish I could learn my tables like Leah. Everybody laughs when I paint. I join in laughing but I get hurt you know. I get really scared when I do my SATs too. . . I'm a real dummy. I would like you to try and help me think of some good things about myself.* Questions: What does she think achievement means? What kind of skills do we need to get along with people? Would it help if ... Ask if any child would like help in reflecting on their achievements.	*On the flipchart:* 'What if I don't think I'm good at my work?' 'What good things can I say about myself?'	To help the students work out that achievements are not only academic, but behavioural etc.	*I know/understand that achievement can be non-academic.* *I can identify non-academic qualities that are achievements.* *I respect and value those achievements.*
6. Game: Touch Red The teacher asks everyone to stand up and asks everyone to touch red. Students must touch red on another person. Lots of variations are possible, e.g. touch a left foot with your right little finger. It can also be done in slow motion.		Fun winding-down game.	*I can work and play co-operatively with others*
7. Celebration Round Each child thinks of the special qualities we need to enjoy a life of quality. It might help if teacher gives some examples of his/her own or encourages the class to give some examples, or to have some examples on the flipchart. Each child is given a bead and asked to think of the quality she/he would like to give to her classmates. A long piece of string starts to go round the circle. Each child puts a bead on and says I give our class ...hope, peace etc. This could be done with a jar of marbles/small stones instead, with each child adding a marble to the jar.	Examples of special qualities on the flipchart. See Appendix 5 for photocopiable homework sheet.	To allow the students to think of what makes their lives worth living, and to make a symbolic gesture of hope for the class by giving their positive quality.	*I know/understand what makes for a quality life.* *I can identify a quality that has made my life more positive.* *I respect and value the need for these positive elements in life.*

17

Primary Transition Lesson 2

AIM: Looking forward – what can I achieve? To develop self-awareness, positive self-esteem and confidence

Process	Resources	Rationale	Knowledge/Skills/Attitude
1. Introduction/recap Remind the students that in the last lesson they looked back at the positive things they have achieved, and go on to say that this lesson is about looking forward. Take in any homework which has been brought back.	*On the flipchart:* 'Moving on to secondary school – looking forward'	To present the aim and to set the lesson in context	*I know/understand* the aim of the lesson
2. Game Ask the children to think of all the different things that they may encounter at secondary school, e.g. new teachers. Divide the class into four groups. Each group needs one piece of paper, a pencil and a clipboard. Choose one child to be the leader of each group. Have a list prepared of ten opportunities children may experience, e.g. new friends, learning a language, new teachers, homework. The four leaders come to the front of the class and the teacher whispers number 1 from the list. The children return to their group and draw the opportunity. The first child to guess the opportunity runs to the teacher for the next item on the list. The first group to draw all ten opportunities is the winner.	*On the flipchart:* 'What will it be like?' Paper, pencils and clipboards.	Ice breaker which begins to look at some of the changes they will encounter.	*I know/understand* some of the changes I will notice. *I can* work in a team.
3. Round I'm looking forward to …	*On the flipchart:* 'Hopes and Fears: What am I looking forward to?'	To encourage the students to take a positive look at the future.	*I can* identify my positive feelings about the future. *I respect and value* my thoughts and feelings and those of others.
4. Silent Statements Stand up and cross the circle if: you're looking forward to making new friends; you're not looking forward to losing old friends; you're looking forward to getting homework; you're not looking forward to getting homework; you're looking forward to having more responsibility; you're not looking forward to having more responsibility; you're looking forward to learning a new language; you're not looking forward to learning a new language;	*On the flipchart:* 'Hopes and Fears: What am I not looking forward to?'	To encourage students to be open about their fears as well as their hopes.	*I know/understand* that I can feel hopeful as well as fearful at the same time. *I can* identify some of my hopes and fears. *I respect and value* my own thoughts and those of others.

Process	Resources	Rationale	Knowledge/Skills/Attitude
4. Silent Statements (continued) you're looking forward to after school clubs; you're looking forward to ... you're not looking forward to .... (Ask the children if they would like to add any of their own)			
5. Open Forum Ask the children if anybody is not looking forward to secondary school. Stress that change can make us feel anxious and scared. Would it help if		To help the young people to realise that no situation is hopeless and to encourage them to help each other with providing possible solutions.	*I know/understand* some of the concerns that I and my peers have about transition. *I can* help others and myself by thinking of solutions to these concerns. *I respect and value* the help others can give me.
6. Game Each child is given a piece of paper. She/he draws four things she is looking forward to in each corner. Instruct the children to draw three things that are true and one that is false. The children pair up with a partner. Label the children A/B. A begins explaining the changes she is looking forward to. B has to work out which change is not true. When each child has had a go they move on to a new partner.	Paper and pencils.	A more private and relaxed opportunity for students to express hopes and concerns.	*I know/understand* what I am not looking forward to. *I can* identify my hopes and concerns with those of other people. *I respect and value* my feelings and those of others.
7. Celebration Round Pass a handshake round the room. Whilst shaking hands, encourage good eye contact and body language, and ask them to say I wish you ... (kindness, encouragement praise etc.), a positive quality which they might have thought about as homework during the week. Point out that these are gifts that we can give to others (pass it on). Homework: see if you can pass it on – show that quality to someone this week.		To encourage a positive attitude towards others, and to realise that if we want a positive world we have a responsibility to be positive to others.	

19

Primary Transition Lesson 3

AIM: To look at what losses and gains I might experience; to develop independence and responsibility

Process	Resources	Rationale	Knowledge/Skills/Attitude
1. Introduction/recap Explain that change involves losses and gains. Give personal example if possible.	*On the flipchart:* 1. 'Losses and gains'	To set the lesson in context.	*I know/understand* the different changes that take place in human life
2. Game: Gunge Tell the children you have a bucket of orange gunge and it's really disgusting! Pull out the orange gunge and throw it at your own face. Then pull it off your face and throw it at one of them. The gunge is passed around/across the circle until everybody has had a face full. They can add disgusting noises if they want.	*On the flipchart:* 2. 'Gunge'	This is a fun game and always helps to start a serious circle time.	*I can* take part in a fun game without embarrassment. I respect and value everybody in my group.
3. Round As this has the potential to be unsafe for some children it might help if they work in pairs. Talk to the children about the losses they might encounter, and to think of all the other primary school children in their area about to take this major new step. I wonder what they are all thinking about when they imagine their new life. I wonder if you can think of all the different losses that both you and other children may be thinking about. Now ask the pairs to complete the round: People might worry about losing... (my old teachers, my old friends, my school uniform, the school, the walk to school etc.)	*On the flipchart:* 3. 'People might worry about losing ...'	To explore the idea of loss.	*I know/understand* the meaning of loss. *I can* imagine and express some of the losses I will experience. *I respect and value* my thoughts and the thoughts of others.
4. Silent Statements Stand up and cross the circle if: you worry about losing your way to school; you worry about losing your books (you have to carry them around!); you're looking forward to having new experiences; you're looking forward to having new friends; you worry about losing your primary school teachers; you're looking forward to getting new teachers; Reflect on the statements. Reassure children that it is perfectly normal to experience two conflicting feelings at the same time. For example, I may look forward to meeting new teachers but I can still feel sad at the loss of former teachers.		To encourage openness about feelings around the losses and gains.	*I know/understand* that with losses come gains and with hopes come fears. *I can* express my hopes and fears. *I respect and value* that others might feel differently from me.

20

Process	Resources	Rationale	Knowledge/Skills/Attitude
5. Open Forum The teacher is in role as a young person voicing thoughts and concerns about the future without their best friend and teacher. The teacher either adapts the following to be used as a letter or she/he uses it as a basis for teacher in role. *By next week it'll all be gone won't it. Miss keeps saying we'll make new friends or we'll get to know smashing new teachers but she's wrong. I don't want new friends or new teachers. I just want....Oh, I don't know what I want . Yes, yes I do! I want everything to stay the same. Same tables, same chairs, same coatpegs, same journey, same lessons, same people. Why doesn't everything just stay the same?* [Shows a photograph of friend] *We've been friends since – since the beginning. Sometimes we argue but we can't stay breaking up for long. Why does she/he have to go to another school – it's not fair! Then today what do I find out, my best teacher is going to New Zealand – she/he's got a new job. She says I can write but I'm not going to – I'm not going to do anything. I'm fed up with everyone.* What does she/he mean: *'It'll all be gone?'* I wonder what life would be like if it always stayed the same? Could it always stay the same? I wonder why humans find change difficult? What positive things might happen through change? How do you recognise when someone is feeling lonely? Will we think to look out for other people's loneliness? Would it help if...?	On the flipchart: 4. 'I like it the way it is' 'Why does it all have to change?' 'Do we know when someone is feeling lonely?'	To help the children consider the sorts of losses they may experience through transition and to think of ways in which they can help themselves and others.	*I know/understand* about some of the losses I will experience. *I can* think of ways to manage those losses and look forward to the positive side of change. *I respect and value* the need for change.
6. Game: People to People Children stand in pairs. The teacher calls out instructions. For example, finger to finger, toe to toe. Each instruction is matched with an action. After four instructions have been called the teacher calls 'People to people' and the children form a new pair.		Fun game which encourages coordination, working with different people and safe physical proximity.	*I can* work with a range of people, and listen to and follow instructions.
7. Ending: Electric Squeeze All hold hands and feel the electric current (the squeeze) go around the circle. People can send the current around in the opposite direction by squeezing twice with the same hand (they are only allowed one turn at this though – why?). Try and do it without it being obvious to see – one person can stand in the middle and try and spot the current passing.	On the flipchart: 5. 'I can work co-operatively with others in a team'	Fun end session requiring concentration: to work co-operatively and show consideration for others.	*I can* work together co-operatively with others. *I respect and value* other people in my group.

21

Primary Transition Lesson 4

AIM: To develop independence and responsibility; dealing with fears

Process	Resources	Rationale	Knowledge/Skills/Attitude
1. Introduction and ground rules Explain what transition is (it means passing from one to another) and that the aim is to help to make it a positive experience.	Appendix 1 (rules). *On the flipchart:* 'Transition – passing from one to the other'	To set the boundaries and explain the reason for the lesson.	*I know/understand* the meaning of transition and the reason for the lesson. *I respect and value* the need for rules.
2. Game: Find someone who ... After the children have played the game the teacher talks briefly about his/her experience of change. Make children aware that it is quite normal to experience negative and positive feelings at the same time. This will have more impact if the teacher can demonstrate through a personal experience, e.g. 'When I got a new job I felt really excited but I was also frightened. Would I be able to do it? What if I made a mistake?'	Appendix 6.	Ice-breaker to raise awareness of some of the issues which will crop up with transition.	*I know/understand* some of the issues which are going to crop up with transition. *I can ask* questions and talk confidently about this with others. *I respect* my thoughts and the thoughts of other people.
3. Round Ask the children to form pairs. Each pair has to complete the following trigger statements: We're looking forward to ... We're not looking forward to ... Write down the worries ready for next lesson.	*On the flipchart:* 'We're looking forward to ...' 'We're not looking forward to ...'	To show that there are positive aspects to change, and to encourage worries and anxieties to be aired.	*I know/understand* some positive and negative sides to transition. *I can express* my hopes and fears *I value* the chance to ...

22

Process	Resources	Rationale	Knowledge/Skills/Attitude
4. Silent Statements Stand up and cross the circle if: you are able to think of a trusted adult you could talk to if things go wrong one day; you like things to stay the same; you can remember your first day at school; you can think of a good way to remember all the things you need for school; you think everyone else looks OK about going to school, it's just you!		To heighten awareness of how transition will feel in a safe and positive way.	*I know/am aware* of how much change affects me. I know I am not alone with these feelings. *I can think of someone* who can help if I need it.
5. Open Forum In role the teacher plays a young person who is scared of going to secondary school because she/he might get bullied. She/he is beginning to have nightmares and doesn't want to go to the taster day. No one else looks scared. 'What is wrong with me?' she asks. Questions: I wonder why she thinks she might get bullied. I wonder what his/her dreams are about. Is there anything wrong with her? I wonder if other young people might feel similar? Then the teacher asks if any of the young people might need help in this area.	*On the flipchart:* 'Is it just me that feels like this?' 'We can help each other'	To help young people look at some of the worries and anxieties around transition using a problem-solving approach.	*I am aware of the* anxiety of being bullied at secondary school. *I can work with others* to allay fears and identify fear-related distortions. *I empathise and* respond sensitively to others in the group.
6. Game This is a game which encourages caring and co-operation. Each child walks around to music with a beanbag on their head. If the beanbag comes off the child has to stand statue still. It is up to other children to 'rescue' the child. They have to bend down, pick up the beanbag and replace it on the child's head.	Beanbags, music source	To encourage care and co-operation in the group.	*I can* be aware of and respond to the needs of others.
7. Celebration Round Work in pairs first. In today's lesson I have learnt that I can ...		To celebrate and affirm the progress which each person has made this lesson.	*I can summarise* something of what I have learnt this lesson. *I respect/value* my contribution to the lesson and the contributions of others.

23

Primary Transition Lesson 5

AIM: To develop independence and responsibility; how can I recognise when I need help?

Process	Resources	Rationale	Knowledge/Skills/Attitude
1. Introduction/recap Teacher to quickly summarise the previous lesson and explain that this one will explore some of the worries and concerns.	*On the flipchart:* AIM: To be independent and responsible.	To show continuity from previous lesson and to clarify aim.	
2. Game: When I leave this class ... The first person begins by saying, 'When I leave this class I will take a ...' (they name something in the classroom, e.g. desk). The second person adds another item, e.g. 'When I leave this class I will take a desk and a ...' This continues around the circle with everybody helping if necessary.	*On the flipchart:* 'When I leave this class ...'	A fun warm-up game with the motto which says you can't take it all with you.	*I can* take part in a whole group exercise. *I can* help others appropriately.
3. Round Ask the children to form pairs. Type the worries from the previous lesson on to card. Make sure children have given permission for you to do this. Each pair looks at the problem and responds with a 'would it help' response. The card is read out and the pair then offer their 'we think it might help if ...' The teacher also adds responses.	Typed-up results from Lesson 4.	To encourage the young people to realise their own problem-solving abilities	*I know* some of the anxieties about the different changes that take place with transition. *I can* work with a partner to find solutions. *I can* respond sensitively to the needs of others.
4. Silent Statements Stand up and cross the circle if: you think young people worry about being bullied when they go to secondary school; you think young people worry about not having friends at secondary school; you think young people worry about the size of their new secondary school; you think young people worry about what their new teachers will be like; you think young people worry about their homework.		To allow the young people to express their own worries.	*I can* express my anxieties about transition.

Process	Resources	Rationale	Knowledge/Skills/Attitude
5. Open Forum In role the teacher plays a young person who is finding the work at secondary school very hard. The young person is not doing their homework and is also getting into trouble for causing distractions during lessons. She/he is occasionally taking time off school to avoid being exposed. Questions: I wonder why the young person causes distractions during the lesson? I wonder how the young person is feeling about her/himself? What might the consequences be if the young person continues to hide his/her problem? What might make this young person want to hide his/her problems? The children are then asked if they can help the young person. The teacher then asks if any of the children might need help in this area.	*On the flipchart:* 'Do I know when I need to ask for help?' 'Who do I ask and how?'	Young people can become aware of how it might be difficult to ask for help in new situations, but not to ask for help could lead to further problems.	*I know* the importance of asking for help. *I can* ask for and offer help. *I can* respond to other people's problems with empathy. I am beginning to take responsibility for myself and for my behaviour.
6. Game: Change Places Everybody in the circle is on their hands and knees. Number the pupils alternately 1 and 2. When your number is called out you move one limb forward. The idea is to get to the other side of the circle. The centre of the circle can become very congested and a great deal of co-operation is needed for the whole class to be successful. Try the game again a second time, this time encouraging skills of co-operation. (Teacher highlights how this game reflects reality.)	*On the flipchart:* 'If we push and ignore others' needs we may be prevented from moving at all. If we co-operate we may all have our needs met.'	To develop the skills of co-operation.	*I am aware* of the benefits of working co-operatively. *I can* work co-operatively with others.
7. Celebration and Affirmation Young people to work in pairs to say something positive about each other. Something positive that my partner has done in this lesson is … Finish with Electric Squeeze – all hold hands and pass the squeeze. Watch the pulse go round the circle.		To summarise and celebrate achievements.	*I am aware* of and can appreciate what I have achieved this lesson *I can* express appreciation of someone else's achievement. *I can* respond sensitively and appropriately to others in the group.

Primary Transition Lesson 6

AIM: Ending and beginning

Process	Resources	Rationale	Knowledge/Skills/Attitude
1. Introduction/recap Teacher to summarise the previous five lessons and to explain this is the last one, and is about moving on.	*On the flipchart:* 'Endings'	To show continuity from previous lesson and to clarify aim.	
2. Game: Interview A volunteer goes out of the room. The group has to decide on a character from secondary school, e.g. geography teacher, lunchtime supervisor. The volunteer returns and 'interviews' members of the group (for which there is only allowed a yes/no answer) in order to find out who the character is.		A game which thinks about the different people there are in secondary school.	
3. Round How are we feeling about moving up to secondary school? I am feeling …	*On the flipchart:* 'How am I feeling?'	Recognising our feelings.	*I am aware* of my feelings.
4. Silent Statements Stand up and cross the circle if: you're looking forward to the summer holiday; you think you'll be thinking about secondary school during the holidays; you've got some plans for the holidays, to keep you occupied; you know how to get your new uniform; you still feel nervous about going to secondary school; you also feel excited about going to secondary school; you feel you know what to do if you have a problem at secondary school; you feel ready to move on to secondary school now.		To allow the young people to express their current state of mind about the transition.	*I can identify* my anxieties and feel ready to tackle the imminence of change.

Process	Resources	Rationale	Knowledge/Skills/Attitude
5. Open Forum Each person to have a piece of paper on which they put their name. They then pass the piece of paper to the person on their left. Each person is then to write something positive about the person on their piece of paper. Explain at the end that each person has learnt these positive qualities over time and they are something we have to give – like a gift – to the people we don't yet know at the new school. Questions: How can we use these gifts with peers that we don't yet know? Our relationship with the teachers may take longer to build because we see them less often – how can we use our gifts with the adults? What would be inappropriate/appropriate use of any of the gifts we have? How do you think adults feel when faced with 30 completely new young people in the class? How could you help? What won't help?	A4 paper, pens.	Building self-esteem and confidence. To think about how we can use our gifts in our new relationships with peers and adults.	I can be positive about the good qualities of others. *I am aware* of the good qualities others see in me. *I can* think of ways to help the new relationships I will be making.
6. Game: 40 ways of getting there Have one spare chair in the circle. One person is asked to get to the chair in any way they choose. As they leave an empty chair behind them, another player is asked to move to this chair but in a different way – hopping, jumping, crawling. Everybody must move differently from the way the others have moved.		Fun way of lightening up the atmosphere.	
7. Celebration and Affirmation I offer the people in this group ... peace, trust, etc. for the future.	Light a candle.	To summarise and celebrate.	*I can* respond sensitively and appropriately to others in the group.

Secondary Transition – Taster Day

AIM: To offer young people an experience of secondary school that will enable them to make a positive start to their new school

Process	Resources	Rationale	Knowledge/Skills/Attitude
1. Welcome and introducing the ground rules Teacher may need to read these out and be aware of special needs.	*On the flipchart:* 'Welcome to …' Ground Rules (from Appendix 1).	To provide a safe, secure environment.	*I know* the ground rules. *I can* follow the ground rules. *I respect and value* other people's need for safety and security.
2. Game: Friendship Bingo Students to find a partner who can answer yes to a question, then write that partner's first name in the answer box. Each question must be answered by a different partner, so there should be ten different names on the list when complete. Sit back in the circle when ready.	*On the flipchart:* 'Getting to know you' and Appendix 7.	Enables students to get to know each other.	*I know* some personal information about other members of the group. *I can ask* questions and listen to responses in an appropriate and sensitive manner. *I respect and value* diversity.
3. Round Students work initially in pairs to respond to the following trigger statements: One thing we're looking forward to … One thing we're worried about …	*On the flipchart:* 'Hopes and Fears'	Enables students to express hopes and fears verbally.	*I know* I am not alone with these feelings. *I can* share these feelings with partner and large group. *I respect and am sensitive* to the feelings of others in the group.

Process	Resources	Rationale	Knowledge/Skills/Attitude
4. Silent Statements Cross the circle if: you walked here this morning; you were nervous before you came; you plan to have packed lunch; you have a brother/sister at this school; you got lost around school; you think you'll miss your old school; you're excited about being here; you've said sorry to someone this week; you've met somebody new today; you've smiled at someone new today.	*On the flipchart:* 'How does it feel to be here?'	To give students the opportunity to express their feelings about being here.	*I know* what I feel about coming to secondary school. *I can* sensitively express my feelings about coming to secondary school. *I respect and value* these feelings and those of others.
5. Open Forum Alleviating concerns about secondary school – I'm not OK, you're OK. Teacher role-plays a student who's feeling lost, e.g. *My name is Alex. I feel really lost around here. Everybody else seems OK. I got lost today then at break I couldn't find anyone to talk to. . .nobody else is like this. I just feel . . . oh I don't know what I feel. I'll never feel OK here. I wish I was back with my mates at my old school. Everything there was cool. I didn't go for my dinner yesterday – couldn't face it. I found a place behind the bins and hid. Why can't I be like everybody else?* Students pretend to be Alex's friends to help solve his/her problems beginning with 'Would it help if I....', 'Would it help if you. ...', and 'Would it help if we ...'. Alex always responds with 'yes (that would help) or 'no' and finishes with 'thank you'.	*On the flipchart:* 'We can sort it out'	Helps alleviate concerns and worries about secondary school.	*I know* that the problems I anticipate can be solved. *I can* get help if I need it when I get to secondary school. *I respect and value* other people's ideas.
6. Game: Point to Point Students work in pairs and follow point to point commands e.g. elbow to foot, where one person's elbow touches another person's foot. More examples: toe to finger, nose to ear, knee to ankle.		Winding-down game about co-operation.	*I can* follow instructions and work with other people. *I respect and value* the people I work with.
7. Round: Celebration Something positive that I have learnt today is ...		Leaving on a positive note.	*I know and can* sensitively express today's positive feelings *I respect and value* my achievements.

29

Transition Session for Parent/Student Group

AIM: To encourage parents and students to be empathic towards each other's change of situation

Process	Resources	Rationale	Knowledge/Skills/Attitude
1. Introduction Explain that the next few months will involve certain adjustments and that the aim of this session is to look at some of the issues involved. My name is …	*On the flipchart:* 'Welcome'	Everyone is aware of what the session is about	*I know/understand* the reason for being here.
2. Game Think of a word associated with the move from primary to secondary. For the anxious or weak of heart, stress that any word will do and that it's not a test! This can be done as a quick round or, for the ambitious, a clapping exercise (e.g. stress clap clap, homework clap clap etc.)		Ice breaker that is theme-based.	*I am* beginning to think about the imminent changes.

3. Round: Jumping into each other's shoes
One thing I think my child will be worrying about is …
One thing I think my parent/carer will be worrying about is …
Questions:
  Did anyone notice anything about what the parents said?
  Did anyone notice anything about what their children said?
	On the flipchart:
	'What are our worries?'
		To encourage everybody to look at the imminent changes through the eyes of their child/parent/carer.	*I can try* to imagine and express the concerns that my child/parent/carer might have.
			I respect and value those concerns.

4. Silent Statements
Cross the circle if:
  you think that parents worry about their children going to secondary school;
  you think your parents worried when they went to secondary school;
  you feel that the young people will need help and support;
  you feel that the parents/carers will need help and support;
  you think that parents/carers need to make changes in their lives when their children go to secondary school;
  if you have had a dream about the changes that are about to happen;
  if you're feeling a bit nervous about the changes;
  if you feel clear about all the changes that are going to occur.
		A deeper look at some of the concerns of transition.	*I know/understand* how I and others feel about transition.
			I can admit to those feelings.
			I respect and value the fact that others might think differently from me.

Process	Resources	Rationale	Knowledge/Skills/Attitude
5. Open Forum *Weighing up Alex's Day* Have a large number of marbles and two receptacles: a positive and a negative one. Label them with a plus and a minus sign. Read out Alex's day and ask people in turn to go round the circle putting a marble in the positive/negative receptacle according to what happens, whether it's a positive or negative experience. Weigh up the balance at the end. Was it a good day? How would it affect Alex's emotional health and self-esteem?	Have Alex's Day (Appendix 4) ready to read out. Marbles + receptacles/jars.	A fun way of looking at what can affect the emotional health of a secondary school student.	*I know/understand how being prepared and calm can affect my self-esteem.* *I can identify experiences which improve or lower self-esteem.* *I respect and value the need for positive behaviour/action.*
6. Round: Celebration Something positive that I would like to contribute to our future together is … (e.g. Coming to parents evening/helping with homework/trying my best etc.)	*On the flipchart:* 'How can we help each other?'		*We can think of ways in which we can support each other in the future.*

Secondary Transition First Day/Lesson 1

AIM: To enable young people to feel positive and supported by all, in their move up to secondary school			
Process	**Resources**	**Rationale**	**Knowledge/Skills/Attitude**
1. Welcome and ground rules	*On the flipchart:* 'Welcome' Ground rules (Appendix 1). Camera.	Students will feel safe and secure with firm boundaries and clear expectations.	*I know/understand* the rules *I can* follow rules *I respect, value* and see the need for rules.
2. Game: Name exercise Students to introduce themselves and say one food they like. The catch is that they have to introduce the person on their right first: 'This is Sarah who likes baked beans and I am David and I like chips.'	*On the flipchart:* 'Getting to know you'	To loosen inhibitions, relax the atmosphere and allow students to introduce each other.	*I can* follow instructions, express myself clearly to others.
3. Round: Pairwork One thing I have enjoyed so far about secondary school is ... One thing I am concerned/worried about is ... (Write down the concerns in preparation for no. 5)	Flipchart for recording things enjoyed and concerns.	To allow the students to celebrate the positive aspects of transition and to develop trust in expressing current concerns.	*I can* identify, express and listen to concerns about transition. *I respect and value* the positive thoughts and anxieties belonging to me and others about transition.
4. Silent Statements Cross the circle if: you lost your way here today/the first morning (well done for getting here!) you thought you would but didn't (well done again!); you're still a little uncomfortable in your school uniform; you're starting to feel comfortable in it; you had a sneaky fashion show with it in front of the mirror during the holidays! you think everybody looks enormous here;	*On the flipchart:* 'How does it feel to be here?'	To help the student identify the many different feelings associated with transition.	*I can* identify and express my feelings about transition. *I respect* the feelings I and others have associated with this new phase of our lives.

Process	Resources	Rationale	Knowledge/Skills/Attitude
4. Silent Statements (continued) you like that grown up feeling at secondary school; you're enjoying having all the different lessons to go to; you like having your own planner; you've crossed the circle because somebody else did! you stayed seated because somebody else did! you're beginning to find your way round school.			
5. Open Forum Can we help each other to find solutions to our problems? Invite responses to individual concerns from no. 3 above. Individuals may field responses. Responses begin with words 'Would it help if (I, you, we etc) … Encourage the problem-holders to thank each respondent, and at the end summarise a course of action.	*On the flipchart:* 'How can we help each other?'	To encourage young people to help each other with and to allay anxieties around transition.	*I know* how to get help with my transition anxieties. *I can* offer help to others. *I respect and value* the help that people have offered to me/others.
6. Game: Dinner A fun game – teacher to go round circle marking groups of four naming the individuals as sausages, beans, eggs, potatoes in turn. Then in groups of four they have two minutes to negotiate with each other and together form the image of dinner on a plate with a comment/caption if they wish. They can use the names given or they may decide to become a different dinner. Other groups could guess what they are.	*On the flipchart:* 'Co-operation game: Sausage, eggs, beans, potatoes' It helps if you have clean floor space.	To encourage co-operation in a fun way.	*I can* work with others. *I respect and value* the thoughts and opinions of others in my group.
7. Celebration Round Something positive that I have learnt in this lesson today is … Take a class photograph in order to make the class card for lesson 6.		To encourage students to think positive thoughts.	*I know, am aware of* and can express the positive aspects of this lesson. *I respect and value* the thoughts of others.

Secondary Transition Lesson 2

AIM: To help the young people be aware of when they need help and how to get it

Process	Resources	Rationale	Knowledge/Skills/Attitude
1. Introduction/recap Explain the aim – do I know when I need help, and do I know how to ask for it? We don't always recognise when it is OK to ask for help, and sometimes we're too embarrassed to ask.	*On the flipchart:* 'How do I know when I need help?'	To provide the students with a clear structure of the lesson.	*I know/understand* the reason for the lesson.
2. Game: Silly Answers One student stands in the middle, while others take turns to ask questions of the person in the middle. The person in the middle gives a silly answer whilst trying not to smile. If they smile, the person who last asked a question takes her/his place.	*On the flipchart:* 'Silly Answers'	Warming up activity which involves asking questions.	I can control my face muscles! I can *also ask questions* in public.
3. Round: Pairwork Remind class of confidentiality rule. 1. When might you need help at secondary school?, and 2. What fears might stop you from asking for help? Encourage students to look at things that they find hard or upsetting. Feed back the answers to the second question. I might not ask for help because ... Write up the different fears.	*On the flipchart:* Questions 1 & 2.	To explore the fears around asking for help, and to examine the ways sensitive others should behave at this time.	*I am aware of/sensitive* to situations where I and others may need help and to the fears involved. *I can express my fears* and listen to other people's fears. *I respect and value* the need for confidentiality.

4. Silent Statements
Cross the circle if:
  you feel confident to ask people for help when you know them;
  you feel less confident to ask people for help when you don't know them;
  you've ever felt embarrassed about having got something wrong;
  you've ever wanted help but have felt too embarrassed/stupid to ask;
  you feel more confident about asking for help when you're not the only one.
	On the flipchart: 'It's OK to make mistakes. It's OK to find things hard'	To raise awareness of the different levels of comfort associated with asking for help.	*I know/am aware* I may have less confidence in new situations.
			I can express these feelings.
			I respect and see the value of openness about these feelings.

Process	Resources	Rationale	Knowledge/Skills/Attitude
5. Open Forum How do we need people to behave towards us when we have these fears? We can help ourselves but sometimes we need people around us and they need us. How do we help Alex? (Teacher to role-play) *I don't like maths. The new teacher – I can't remember his name – is always being unfair to me. I did try at first but I can't do the work so I just chat or doodle. I got a detention last lesson. He doesn't explain it properly. I can't understand the questions that are written down – I'm not a very good reader. I took the homework to my Mum but she didn't have time because she had to go to work and then she said she wouldn't understand it anyway – maths has changed since she went to school. I don't like asking for help because I feel stupid. Nobody else asks for help. I know I'm going to end up being put down a set.* Ask the students to offer help using the words 'would it help if...' Thank each offer of help and state whether this would be useful or not and why. Summarise a plan of action through the help given. It should include talking to parents and asking them to contact the school to ask for help. Further questions: How does Alex feel? What kind of comments from people (friends or family) might improve or ruin his/her confidence? What would happen if Alex did not ask for help? Does the same apply to other sorts of problems?	*On the flipchart:* 'We can help people but they must be able to trust us' and … 'You're OK, I'm not OK' and … 'If I ask for help I can prevent things from getting worse'	To engage students in a problem-solving exercise that explores issues around needing help, what happens when we don't get it or people don't listen, and the importance of persistence.	*I know of* ways to respond to those fears around asking for help. *I can* help others. *I understand* how not asking for help can lead to more problems.
6. Round: Pairwork Sometimes when we're upset or anxious, the words can come out all wrong, or they might not come at all. This can either rub people up the wrong way, or people may not even realise we need help. In pairs think of how you behave when you're anxious or upset and how you can control this. When I'm upset or angry I … One way I can stay in control is …	*On the flipchart:* 'When I'm upset or angry I …' 'One way I can stay in control is …'	Raise awareness of how anxiety can sometimes prevent us from communicating effectively.	*I am aware* how anxiety can prevent me from being understood. *I can* identify solutions to this.
7. Game: Electric Squeeze All hold hands and watch the electric pulse (hand squeeze) pass round the circle. Two squeezes mean change of direction. One person could be 'on' and go outside the room while the class choose a person to be responsible for the change. The volunteer returns and has to watch and try to catch who it is.		Warming-down exercise.	*I can* enjoy working in a team.

Secondary Transition Lesson 3

AIM: to help the young people become aware of the losses and gains associated with transition

Process	Resources	Rationale	Knowledge/Skills/Attitude
1. Introduction/recap The lesson is to help people to get to know and trust one another some more, and to explore awareness of losses and gains so far.	*On the flipchart:* 'Losses and Gains'	To clarify aims and purpose of lesson.	
2. Warm up All members to think of an adjective that begins with the same letter as their forename, and to introduce themselves in turn. e.g. 'active Angelica'.		A fun way to start the lesson, encouraging people to be positive about themselves.	*I can say something positive/fun about myself.*
3. Round Explain to the group that transitions involve losses and gains, and that this transition will mean personal losses and gains for everybody. It helps if teacher can relate a personal experience such as moving on to a new job, or new house. One thing I miss about my old school is … One thing I have gained in my new school is … Or … one thing that I am doing more of and one thing I am doing less of since coming to secondary school is … Or … one feeling I have about my old school/new school now is …	*On the flipchart:* <u>'Transition'</u> Have ready the losses/gains sentence stems.	To allow the student to explore feelings around losses and gains in relation to old and new schools.	*I know and am aware of my feelings around loss associated with transition.* *I can express those feelings.* *I respect and value my and others' feelings and thoughts about this.*
4. Silent Statements Cross the circle if: you think you can find your way round school now; you feel there are good things about being at the new school; you've talked about your new school to someone at home; you've felt tired this last week; you feel there are some 'not so good' things about being at the new school; you are missing your old school and teachers; you've walked past your old school since you've moved to secondary school (did it/would it feel strange?); you've been back to see your old teachers (how did that/would that feel?)		To explore feelings about the change and raise awareness of how many feelings people have in common.	*I am aware that I am not alone with my feelings around transition.* *I respect the feelings of others if they are different from my own.*

Process	Resources	Rationale	Knowledge/Skills/Attitude
5. Open Forum Scenario no. 1 from Appendix 8 or students can be asked to bring any particular problem to the group – it could be the way somebody is treating them, or that they are missing someone, or that they keep losing their temper, or they're finding the work too hard. Remind them of the rules, particularly the rule which does not allow names to be mentioned. Please also see notes on Open Forum in introduction.	Appendix 8, no. 1.	To provide an opportunity to share problems and help each other.	*I know, respect and value* my and others' feelings around loss and gain at transition. *I can express those* feelings, listen to the feelings of others and offer help.
6. Game: Rainbow People are labelled one of four colours. One chair is removed. Person in middle calls a colour and all of that colour cross the circle. Person left in middle calls. Rainbow = all colours cross the circle.		A warming-down activity.	*I can work/have fun with* others whilst respecting and being sensitive to their needs.
7. Round Something positive that I have learnt about myself today is …		To leave on a positive note and to sum up.	*I am sensitive to, value and* can express my developing inner self.

Secondary Transition Lesson 4

AIM: To look at expectations around the subject of transition

Process	Resources	Rationale	Knowledge/Skills/Attitude
1. Introduction/recap Explain that the aim is to raise awareness about some of the difficult issues around transition, looking at what a range of people expect from new students at school and what the students themselves feel.	*On the flipchart:* 'Expectations'	The student will understand the aim of the lesson.	*I know/understand* the reason for this lesson.
2. Game: Noise Three people are chosen as callers and three as receivers, both groups to stand outside the circle opposite each other. Callers secretly decide on a message to send to the receivers. They have two minutes to get the message across. Teacher could provide the message. Remainder of class to distract with noise etc. to prevent message being sent – no physical interference though. To pass message callers can mime, shout louder etc. Allow other people to take a turn.		Fun warm-up game reducing inhibitions and involving teamwork.	*I can* work with others to achieve a purpose.
3. Round Students to work in pairs for two minutes to help each other to come up with a response: 'Now I'm at secondary school I feel people expect me to be ...'. Write the comments up on the flipchart if there is time and invite comments on any changes from the primary setting.	*On the flipchart:* 'People expect me to be ...'	To explore what people expect of us at secondary school and whether it's any different from primary school.	*I can* identify ways in which expectations of me have changed with transition.
4. Silent Statements Cross the circle if (you feel that): you've had an argument with an adult in the morning; you're expected to be more responsible now you're at secondary school; what you want and what adults want for you are sometimes different; you're sometimes still treated too much like a child; you sometimes behave like an adult; you sometimes behave like a child (be honest! – remind them that adults do too); you think you're expected to remember more now you're at secondary school; you get more freedom now you're at secondary school; you wish you were given more freedom;		To explore some of the conflicting aspects of growing up, in terms of expectations.	*I am aware* of the positive and negative effects of expectations from different people. *I value* those expectations which are to improve my well-being.

Process	Resources	Rationale	Knowledge/Skills/Attitude
4. Silent Statements (continued) you're expected to fit more things into your life now you're secondary; you've found yourself running out of time a lot more than before; you're expected to help round the house more as you get older; you feel you're expected to know more than you do.			
5. Open Forum – Alex *I'm really fed up. People expect me to do things all the time. I never have any time to myself now. I'm always having arguments with my Dad because I haven't done things like tidy my room or clear up after myself. I can't be bothered with it all. Last night I had three lots of homework which teachers are expecting today and I haven't done all of it because some of it was set last week and I forgot. I was doing other things last night and then I didn't want to miss the football on TV. Then Dad was on at me for getting up late this morning and not having my bag packed. Why don't they just all leave me alone.* Encourage responses 'Would it help if ...' What does Dad expect of Alex? Is he being unfair? Why can't Alex be bothered with it all? What is she/he feeling about her/himself? What does Alex expect of her/himself? What does Alex need help with? What could happen to Alex if she/he does not get any help? The teacher can draw attention to the words on the flipchart at the end to help summarise the situation.	*On the flipchart:* 1. It feels like people expect too much from me 2. Thinking ahead 3. What do I expect of myself? 4. I can try my best and no more	To seek solutions for a person experiencing difficulties with new expectations and routines.	*I know/understand* how I might not meet other people's expectations. I can find ways of dealing with this. *I respect* the need to communicate politely.
6. Game: I love you honey but I just can't smile Teacher turns to neighbour on left, looks into his/her eyes and says, 'I love you honey', trying to make them laugh. Neighbour responds (without smiling), 'I love you honey, but I just can't smile'. Neighbour then repeats this to person on their left.		Fun anti-inhibition game with positive communication and eye contact.	*I can* use positive eye contact and body language.
7. Round: Celebration Something positive that I expect from myself is ...	*On the flipchart:* 'I can expect good things from myself'	Recognising that we can have our own personal goals.	*I value and can express* positive expectations I have of myself.

39

Secondary Transition Lesson 5

AIM: To look at how friendships might affect me

Process	Resources	Rationale	Knowledge/Skills/Attitude
1. Introduction/recap Teacher to explain that the aim of this lesson is to explore how friendships grow and change, how natural this is, what to expect and how to cope with the changes.	*On the flipchart:* 'Change in friendship'	Setting the scene.	*I know/understand* the reason for the lesson.
2. Game: Elephant, Palm Tree and Aeroplane Everybody stands up. One person stands in the middle and points to someone in the circle, saying elephant/palm tree/aeroplane. To make an elephant the person pointed to leans forward, swinging arms forward to make a trunk. The people on the immediate left and right makes the elephant's ears by creating a circle with their arms and leaning towards the person with the trunk. To make a palm tree the person pointed to stands with arms straight up (the trunk) while the people on either side use their arms to be the fronds coming out of the trunk. To make an aeroplane, the person pointed to stretches their arms out horizontally for the wings while the people on either side bob down to become the engines.		This is a fun warm-up game which requires a lot of concentration.	*I can* work and co-operate with others.
3. Round Teacher to explain that although friendships do sometimes go wrong, they are extremely valuable. When things do go wrong, it can be devastating. Think about a time when you have had a friendship problem. When friendships go wrong I feel ... Comment – how many of those feelings expressed are the same as those associated with loss that we covered in lesson 3.	*On the flipchart:* 'When friendships go wrong I feel ...'	To recognise the feelings around friendship problems.	*I know/understand* the many feelings associated with friendship problems. *I can* openly express those feelings.
4. Silent Statements Stand up and cross the circle if: you came from primary school with friends; you knew someone already at the secondary school; you have already made some new friends; you have noticed your old friends making new friends; there are friends in this class whom you would like to be able to trust; you have ever gone around in a crowd; you ever had someone you have thought of as a best friend;		To help students raise awareness of their present friendship situations and how their needs reflect the needs of others.	*I know/understand* and *can express* feelings about my present friendship situations. *I respect and value* the friendship of other people in this group.

Process	Resources	Rationale	Knowledge/Skills/Attitude
4. Silent Statements (continued) you have ever felt let down and hurt by a friend; a friend has ever felt you had let them down; you forgive people easily; someone has ever forgiven you; you think it's better to sort arguments out rather than let them carry on; you've ever felt left out; you think it possible to have a lot of good friends.			
5. Open Forum Scenario 3 in Appendix 8. Questions: How is Alex feeling? What do you think Alex's friend is thinking? What do you think the third friend is thinking? Does Alex need to feel left out? How should Alex deal with seeing a close friend make new friends? Should/could the two others have behaved more sensitively?	*On the flipchart:* 'Old friends and new friends – is it possible to have both without upsetting either?'	To encourage the students to resolve a new friend–old friend difficulty using a win–win approach.	*I know/understand* the potential difficulties attached to making new friends and of keeping and sharing old friends. *I can respond* maturely to friends enjoying being with others. I respect and value my friends' needs to develop friendships with others.
6. Game: Touchdown Teacher shouts out a number and in pairs, students co-operate to touch the floor with that number of body parts, e.g. three could be three feet with one person holding one leg up in the air. Each set of pairs should try to be different from the rest.		Co-operation exercise.	*I can* co-operate and work with a partner.
7. Celebration Round Students may need time in pairs to prepare this. When I'm a good friend I ...		Students can think about their own 'giving' within friendships.	*I know and can express* the positive friendship qualities I have.

Secondary Transition Lesson 6

AIM: How am I doing so far?

Process	Resources	Rationale	Knowledge/Skills/Attitude
1. Introduction/recap Explain to the students that this lesson is to reflect on all that has happened since they arrived at secondary school, and to celebrate the positive gains and achievements so far. Also, the aim is to look at what they found difficult, and to try to feel more comfortable with that.	*On the flipchart:* 'How am I doing so far?'	To encourage the students to reflect positively on the transitional process they have gone through.	*I know/understand* that change can be difficult but it can bring positive gains. *I can* reflect on the progress that I have made and can allow myself to make mistakes. *I respect and value* my achievements.
2. Game: Our World Put several sheets of newspaper on the ground. The students walk, swim, float around the room until a given signal. At this point every one must stand on a piece of the world. The students continue moving and the process is repeated, each time a piece of the world being taken. Eventually only one or two pieces of the world are left. No student must be left outside when the time for standing on a piece of the world comes. It can be done if everyone co-operates together. Questions: What helped? What didn't help? Did any part of the game remind you of any feelings/thoughts you've had since you've started secondary school?	Newspaper.	Working together, co-operation, and working towards a common aim.	*I respect and value* the need to think about others in order to achieve a win–win situation.
3. Round Close your eyes and think back to the very first day – think of coming through the school gates ... your very first lesson ... your very first meal ... the first piece of homework you received ... the first person you spoke to. In pairs, students to think of two things they have both found difficult. We found it difficult to ...	*On the flipchart:* 'We found it difficult to ...'	Students can not only express the difficult aspects of secondary school, but discover they are not alone with some of those feelings.	*I know/understand* that I have not been on my own in finding certain things difficult. *I can* express the things I have found difficult. *I respect and value* my thoughts and those of others.

Process	Resources	Rationale	Knowledge/Skills/Attitude

4. Silent Statements
Stand up and cross the circle if:
  you have found it hard getting up earlier in the morning;
  you have got used to getting up earlier now;
  you have found it hard getting used to all the different teachers;
  you feel you're getting used to all the different teachers;
  you're used to the new routines of secondary school;
  you think you can remember most of your school timetable now;
  you are using your planner every day;
  you are mostly remembering to bring the things you need;
  you are pleased with the new friends you are making;
  you are enjoying most of your lessons;
  you feel you're a different person now than before the summer holidays;
  you feel to have learnt a lot about 'life' since primary school.
	On the flipchart:
	'We have coped with change'
	'We have achieved!'
		To help the young people to realise how much they have learnt through the process of change.	*I know/understand that* I have done well making adjustments to my new lifestyle.
			I can survive change.

5. Open Forum: Star Students Cut out the printed stars from the appendix, and display in the middle of the circle. Ask the students in pairs to select two stars that best match their mutual feelings and thoughts. When they have chosen their stars they return to sit in the circle. When all students have chosen their stars, two by two the students read out their stars and place them on a sheet of paper in the middle of the circle. This continues until all students have had a turn. The teacher encourages all the students to reflect on the importance of the process through which they have gone. The completed sheet can be displayed as a symbol of the students' positive achievements in their form rooms.	See Appendix 9.	To help the students to recognise that purely through coping with change, they have already achieved much of value since their arrival at secondary school.	*I know/understand how* change can be positive. *I can work with* someone to identify some of the positive achievements we have in common. *I respect and value* my thoughts and those of others.
6. Game: Pretzel All except for two in the group, hold hands in a line. The leader leads the group by hand, twisting and weaving under arms and through people without letting go of hands until the group is tangled. The two remaining people are the untanglers who advise how to unknot the group.		A fun warming-down exercise.	*I can work with* others and have fun.
7. Celebration Round Our team has done well because ... Teacher then gives out a celebration card to each student.	To make celebration cards see note at the end of Appendix 9.	To give the teacher a chance to personally congratulate each person.	*I feel respected and valued* by the teacher.

Bibliography and Further Reading

Canter, L. and Canter, M. (1976) **Assertive Discipline: A Take Charge Approach for Today's Educator** Canter and Associates, Seal Beach, California

Curry M. and Bromfield C. (1998) **Circle Time: In-service Manual** National Association for Special Educational Needs, Tamworth

Department for Education and Employment (1999) **Social Inclusion - Pupil Support: draft guidance** DfEE London

Dewar, R., Palser, K. and Notley, M. (1989) **Games Games Games II** The Woodcraft Folk, London

Edinburgh Family Service Unit **The Primary/Secondary Transition Programme**

Egan, G. (1975) **The Skilled Helper** Brookes Cole, Monterey, California

Gardner, H. (1993) **Multiple Intelligence: The Theory in Practice** Basic Books

Goleman, D. (1996) **Emotional Intelligence: Why it matters more than IQ** Bloomsbury Publishing, London

Inman, S. and Buck, M., ed. (1995) **Adding Value? Schools' Responsibility for the Personal Development of Pupils** Trentham Books

Korb-Khalsa, K. L. (1996) **Life Management Skills** Wellness Reproductions Inc, Ohio

Maslow, A. H. (1962) **Towards a Psychology of Being** Van Nostrand Reinholt, New York

McNamara, S. and Moreton G. (1995) **Changing Behaviour** David Fulton Publishers, London

Mitchell, G. (1997) **Practical Strategies for Individual Behaviour Difficulties** David Fulton Publishers, London

Mosley, J. (1993) **Turn Your School Round** LDA, Cambridge

Mosley, J. (1996) **Quality Circle Time in the Primary Classroom** LDA, Cambridge

Mosley, J. (1998) **More Quality Circle Time** LDA, Cambridge

Mosley, J. and Tew, M. (1999) **Quality Circle Time in the Secondary School: A Handbook of Good Practice** David Fulton Publishers, London

National Open College Network **Key Skills (communication, working with others etc)** NOCN, Derby, course information

Newcastle upon Tyne LEA (1987) **Co-operating for a Change**

Pax Christi (1997) **Winners All: Co-operative Games for All Ages** Stanhope Press, London

Peace Pledge Union (1993) **Co-operative Games: Activities for a Peaceful World** London

Powell, T. (1992) **The Mental Health Handbook** Winslow Press, London

Qualifications and Curriculum Authority (1998) **Initial Report on Education for Citizenship and the Teaching of Democracy in Schools** QCA, London

Rogers, C. (1961) **On Becoming a Person** Houghton Mifflin, Boston

Rogers, C. (1978) **On Personal Power** Constable and Co., London

Salovey, P. and Sluyter, D. J. (1997) **Emotional Development and Emotional Intelligence** Basic Books, USA

Smith, A. (1996) **Accelerated Learning in the Classroom** Network Educational Press, Stafford

Tattum, D. and Herbert, G. (1993) **Countering Bullying: Initiatives by Schools and Local Authorities** Trentham Books, Stoke on Trent

appendices

(photocopiable resources)

Circle Time Rules

(Respect)

1. Listen to others

(Respect)
2. Be helpful

(Respect)
3. Avoid put downs

(Respect)
4. No naming

appendix 2

Self-evaluation sheet for teachers starting circle time

1. Did I start the lesson in a calm ordered way?	yes ☐	no ☐
2. Was the room organised for the beginning of the lesson?	yes ☐	no ☐
3. Was there enough structure to the lesson:	yes ☐	no ☐
● Ground rules	yes ☐	no ☐
● Skill awareness	yes ☐	no ☐
● Game	yes ☐	no ☐
● Round	yes ☐	no ☐
● Open Forum	yes ☐	no ☐
● Game	yes ☐	no ☐
● Round	yes ☐	no ☐
4. What was achieved?		
● The Aim	yes ☐	no ☐
● Knowledge	yes ☐	no ☐
● Skills	yes ☐	no ☐
● Attitudes	yes ☐	no ☐
5. Did students get the opportunity to ask for help themselves?	yes ☐	no ☐
6. Did I show encouragement to shy students?	yes ☐	no ☐
7. The right to pass - was this observed, and were students given a second chance?	yes ☐	no ☐
8. Did I follow my circle time rules?	yes ☐	no ☐
9. Did I encourage the positive use of rules through;	yes ☐	no ☐
● praise	yes ☐	no ☐
● tangible paper reward	yes ☐	no ☐
● eliciting peer praise	yes ☐	no ☐
10. Did I follow my own pre-arranged sanction rules?	yes ☐	no ☐
11. Did I arrange with another teacher where any child who uses up all sanctions could be removed to another class?	yes ☐	no ☐
12. Have I recorded my assessments?	yes ☐	no ☐
13. Have I taken time to follow up students who have asked for help in the open forum?	yes ☐	no ☐

Name

Date

Student Log

Transition - Circle Work

Primary Session no. 1
Looking back - what have I achieved?

How did I do?

Self Assessment

---

1. Rules: How did I get on with . . .

a) respecting others (examples of non-respect: interrupting, put downs, inappropriate laughter or naming someone)?

☐ 1 ☐ 2 ☐ 3 ☐ 4 ☐ 5

b) listening to what everybody else had to say?

☐ 1 ☐ 2 ☐ 3 ☐ 4 ☐ 5

c) respecting group confidentiality over the week?

☐ 1 ☐ 2 ☐ 3 ☐ 4 ☐ 5

2. Game

a) What did I say for my achievement?

b) What else could I have said?

3. Round: What did I say?

Something I have learnt that I really value is . . .

Did I want to say anything else?

4. Silent Statement (did I cross the circle?)

a) if you remember learning to tie your shoe laces ☐ yes ☐ no

b) if you remember learning how to make friends ☐ yes ☐ no

c) if you remember hurting someone and learning how to say sorry ☐ yes ☐ no

d) if you remember lying about something and having to learn about being honest ☐ yes ☐ no

e) if you remember finding something difficult to learn ☐ yes ☐ no

5. Open Forum: A child cannot remember any positive achievements
   What did I say?

a) Would it help if

b) Something I could have said but didn't:

6. Game

a) Did I join in?   ☐ yes   ☐ no

b) Did I listen to and follow instructions?   ☐ yes   ☐ no

7. Round: What did I say?

The quality I gave to the class was

Something else I could have said:

8. Overall Performance

How did I get on with:

a) being honest about my feelings?   ☐ 1 ☐ 2 ☐ 3 ☐ 4 ☐ 5

b) speaking clearly?   ☐ 1 ☐ 2 ☐ 3 ☐ 4 ☐ 5

c) feeling OK about making mistakes?   ☐ 1 ☐ 2 ☐ 3 ☐ 4 ☐ 5

d) not laughing when other people seem to be making mistakes?   ☐ 1 ☐ 2 ☐ 3 ☐ 4 ☐ 5

e) not feeling embarrassed to speak out?   ☐ 1 ☐ 2 ☐ 3 ☐ 4 ☐ 5

f) giving positive help to other people when they get stuck?   ☐ 1 ☐ 2 ☐ 3 ☐ 4 ☐ 5

9. Did I . . .

a) give a warm signal to anyone?   ☐ yes   ☐ no

b) receive a warm signal from anyone?   ☐ yes   ☐ no

Teacher comment

Name ( ) Date ( )

Student Log

Primary Session no. 2
Looking forward - what can I achieve?

How did I do? **Self Assessment**

---

1. Rules: How did I get on with . . .

a) respecting others (examples of non-respect: interrupting, put downs, inappropriate laughter or naming someone)?
☐ 1 ☐ 2 ☐ 3 ☐ 4 ☐ 5

b) listening to what everybody else had to say?
☐ 1 ☐ 2 ☐ 3 ☐ 4 ☐ 5

c) respecting group confidentiality over the week?
☐ 1 ☐ 2 ☐ 3 ☐ 4 ☐ 5

2. Game

a) Did I work well with my team? ☐ yes ☐ no

b) Did I behave positively towards others? ☐ yes ☐ no

3. Round: What did I say? I'm looking forward to . . .

( )

Did I want to say anything else?

( )

4. Silent Statement (did I cross the circle?)

a) if you're looking forward to making new friends ☐ yes ☐ no
b) if you're not looking forward to losing old friends ☐ yes ☐ no
c) if you're looking forward to getting homework ☐ yes ☐ no
d) if you're not looking forward to getting homework ☐ yes ☐ no
e) if you're looking forward to having more responsibility ☐ yes ☐ no
f) if you're not looking forward to having more responsibility ☐ yes ☐ no
g) if you're looking forward to learning a new language ☐ yes ☐ no
h) if you're not looking forward to learning a new language ☐ yes ☐ no
i) if you're looking forward to after school clubs ☐ yes ☐ no
j) if you're looking forward to . . ☐ yes ☐ no
k) if you're not looking forward to . . ☐ yes ☐ no

5. Open Forum: What did I say?

a) Would it help if . . ?

b) Something I could have said but didn't:

6. Game: True or False

a) Did I guess correctly? ☐ yes ☐ no

b) Did I find I felt the same as others? ☐ yes ☐ no

7. Round: What did I say?

Which quality did you wish other people had?

Something else I could have said:

8. Overall Performance

How did I get on with:

a) being honest about my feelings? ☐ 1 ☐ 2 ☐ 3 ☐ 4 ☐ 5

b) speaking clearly? ☐ 1 ☐ 2 ☐ 3 ☐ 4 ☐ 5

c) feeling OK about making mistakes? ☐ 1 ☐ 2 ☐ 3 ☐ 4 ☐ 5

d) not laughing when other people seem to be making mistakes? ☐ 1 ☐ 2 ☐ 3 ☐ 4 ☐ 5

e) not feeling embarrassed to speak out? ☐ 1 ☐ 2 ☐ 3 ☐ 4 ☐ 5

f) giving positive help to other people when they get stuck? ☐ 1 ☐ 2 ☐ 3 ☐ 4 ☐ 5

9. Did I . . .

a) give a warm signal to anyone? ☐ yes ☐ no

b) receive a warm signal from anyone? ☐ yes ☐ no

Teacher comment

Name ⟨ ⟩ Date ⟨ ⟩

Student Log

Transition - Circle Work

Primary Session no. 3
Losses and Gains

How did I do?   **Self Assessment**

---

1. Rules: How did I get on with . . .

a) respecting others (examples of non-respect: interrupting, put downs, inappropriate laughter or naming someone)?   ☐ 1 ☐ 2 ☐ 3 ☐ 4 ☐ 5

b) listening to what everybody else had to say?   ☐ 1 ☐ 2 ☐ 3 ☐ 4 ☐ 5

c) respecting group confidentiality over the week?   ☐ 1 ☐ 2 ☐ 3 ☐ 4 ☐ 5

2. Game

a) Did I make disgusting noises?   ☐ yes   ☐ no

b) Did I enjoy the idea?   ☐ yes   ☐ no

c) Did I join in without embarrassment?   ☐ yes   ☐ no

3. Round: What did I say?   People might worry about losing . . .

⟨ ⟩

Did I want to say anything else?

⟨ ⟩

4. Silent Statement (did I cross the circle?)

a) if you worry about losing your way to school   ☐ yes   ☐ no

b) if you worry about losing your books (you have to carry them around!)   ☐ yes   ☐ no

c) if you're looking forward to having new experiences   ☐ yes   ☐ no

d) if you're looking forward to having new friends   ☐ yes   ☐ no

e) if you worry about losing your primary school teachers   ☐ yes   ☐ no

f) if you're looking forward to getting new teachers   ☐ yes   ☐ no

5. Open Forum: The young person who is losing best friend/teacher
   What did I say?

a) Would it help if . . .

⟨ ⟩

b) Something I could have said but didn't:

⟨ ⟩

6. Game:

a) Did I join in?   ☐ yes   ☐ no

b) Did I work together co-operatively with someone?   ☐ yes   ☐ no

7. Overall Performance

How did I get on with:

a) being honest about my feelings?   ☐ 1 ☐ 2 ☐ 3 ☐ 4 ☐ 5

b) speaking clearly?   ☐ 1 ☐ 2 ☐ 3 ☐ 4 ☐ 5

c) feeling OK about making mistakes?   ☐ 1 ☐ 2 ☐ 3 ☐ 4 ☐ 5

d) not laughing when other people seem to be making mistakes?   ☐ 1 ☐ 2 ☐ 3 ☐ 4 ☐ 5

e) not feeling embarrassed to speak out?   ☐ 1 ☐ 2 ☐ 3 ☐ 4 ☐ 5

f) giving positive help to other people when they get stuck?   ☐ 1 ☐ 2 ☐ 3 ☐ 4 ☐ 5

8. Did I . . .

a) give a warm signal to anyone?   ☐ yes   ☐ no

b) receive a warm signal from anyone?   ☐ yes   ☐ no

Teacher comment

Name ( ) Date ( )

Student Log

Transition - Circle Work

Primary Session no. 4
Dealing with fears

How did I do?
Self Assessment

---

1. Rules: How did I get on with . . .

a) respecting others (examples of non-respect: interrupting, put downs, inappropriate laughter or naming someone)?

☐ 1 ☐ 2 ☐ 3 ☐ 4 ☐ 5

b) listening to what everybody else had to say?
☐ 1 ☐ 2 ☐ 3 ☐ 4 ☐ 5

c) respecting group confidentiality over the week?
☐ 1 ☐ 2 ☐ 3 ☐ 4 ☐ 5

2. Game

a) Did I find people who felt the same as me? ☐ yes ☐ no

b) Did I find it helpful to know that others feel the same as me? ☐ yes ☐ no

c) Did I speak politely to others? ☐ yes ☐ no

3. Round: What did we say?

We're looking forward to . . .

( )

We're not looking forward to . . .

( )

4. Silent Statement (did I cross the circle?)

a) if you could think of a trusted adult ☐ yes ☐ no

b) if you like things to stay the same ☐ yes ☐ no

c) if you remember your first day at school ☐ yes ☐ no

d) if you think of a good way to remember all the things you need for school ☐ yes ☐ no

e) if you think everyone else looks OK about going to school, it's just you ☐ yes ☐ no

5. Open Forum: The young person frightened of being bullied. What did I say?

a) Would it help if . . .

( )

b) Something I could have said but didn't:

( )

58

6. Game

a) Did I join in?   ☐ yes   ☐ no

b) Did I rescue others?   ☐ yes   ☐ no

7. Round: What did I say?

In today's lesson I have learnt that I can . . .

Something else I could have said:

8. Overall Performance

How did I get on with:

a) being honest about my feelings?   ☐ 1 ☐ 2 ☐ 3 ☐ 4 ☐ 5

b) speaking clearly?   ☐ 1 ☐ 2 ☐ 3 ☐ 4 ☐ 5

c) feeling OK about making mistakes?   ☐ 1 ☐ 2 ☐ 3 ☐ 4 ☐ 5

d) not laughing when other people seem to be making mistakes?   ☐ 1 ☐ 2 ☐ 3 ☐ 4 ☐ 5

e) not feeling embarrassed to speak out?   ☐ 1 ☐ 2 ☐ 3 ☐ 4 ☐ 5

f) giving positive help to other people when they get stuck?   ☐ 1 ☐ 2 ☐ 3 ☐ 4 ☐ 5

9. Did I . . .

a) give a warm signal to anyone?   ☐ yes   ☐ no

b) receive a warm signal from anyone?   ☐ yes   ☐ no

Teacher comment

Name ( ) Date ( )

Student Log   **Transition - Circle Work**

Primary Session no. 5
How can I recognise when I need help?

How did I do?   **Self Assessment**

---

1. Rules: How did I get on with . . .

a) respecting others (examples of non-respect: interrupting, put downs, inappropriate laughter or naming someone)?   ☐ 1 ☐ 2 ☐ 3 ☐ 4 ☐ 5

b) listening to what everybody else had to say?   ☐ 1 ☐ 2 ☐ 3 ☐ 4 ☐ 5

c) respecting group confidentiality over the week?   ☐ 1 ☐ 2 ☐ 3 ☐ 4 ☐ 5

2. Game
When I leave this class I will take a . . .

( )

3. Round: What did I say?
What was the worry?

( )

How did I answer it?

( )

4. Silent Statement (did I cross the circle?)

a) if you think young people worry about being bullied when they go to secondary school   ☐ yes   ☐ no

b) if you think young people worry about not having friends at secondary school   ☐ yes   ☐ no

c) if you think young people worry about the size of their new secondary school   ☐ yes   ☐ no

d) if you think young people worry about what their new teachers will be like   ☐ yes   ☐ no

e) if you think young people worry about their homework   ☐ yes   ☐ no

5. Open Forum

Somebody at secondary school is finding work very hard. What did I say?

a) Would it help if . . .

( )

b) Something I could have said but didn't:

( )

6. Game

a) Did I work co-operatively the first time?   ☐ yes   ☐ no

b) Did I work co-operatively the second time?   ☐ yes   ☐ no

7. Round: What did I say?

Something positive that my partner has done this lesson:

Something somebody said about me:

8. Overall Performance

How did I get on with:

a) being honest about my feelings?   ☐ 1 ☐ 2 ☐ 3 ☐ 4 ☐ 5

b) speaking clearly?   ☐ 1 ☐ 2 ☐ 3 ☐ 4 ☐ 5

c) feeling OK about making mistakes?   ☐ 1 ☐ 2 ☐ 3 ☐ 4 ☐ 5

d) not laughing when other people seem to be making mistakes?   ☐ 1 ☐ 2 ☐ 3 ☐ 4 ☐ 5

e) not feeling embarrassed to speak out?   ☐ 1 ☐ 2 ☐ 3 ☐ 4 ☐ 5

f) giving positive help to other people when they get stuck?   ☐ 1 ☐ 2 ☐ 3 ☐ 4 ☐ 5

9. Did I . . .

a) give a warm signal to anyone?   ☐ yes   ☐ no

b) receive a warm signal from anyone?   ☐ yes   ☐ no

Teacher comment

Name ⟨   ⟩   Date ⟨   ⟩

Student Log

Primary Session no. 6
Ending and beginning

How did I do?   **Self Assessment**

---

1. Rules: How did I get on with . . .

a) respecting others (examples of non-respect: interrupting, put downs, inappropriate laughter or naming someone)?
☐ 1 ☐ 2 ☐ 3 ☐ 4 ☐ 5

b) listening to what everybody else had to say?   ☐ 1 ☐ 2 ☐ 3 ☐ 4 ☐ 5

c) respecting group confidentiality over the week?   ☐ 1 ☐ 2 ☐ 3 ☐ 4 ☐ 5

2. Game
a) Did I work well with others in the class?

⟨   ⟩

b) Did I not give the game away?

⟨   ⟩

3. Round: What did I say?

How are you feeling about moving up to secondary school?

I am feeling . . .

⟨   ⟩

Did I want to say anything else?

⟨   ⟩

4. Silent Statement (did I cross the circle?)

a) if you're looking forward to the summer holiday   ☐ yes ☐ no
b) if you think you'll be thinking about secondary school during the holidays   ☐ yes ☐ no
c) if you've got some plans for the holidays, to keep you occupied   ☐ yes ☐ no
d) if you know how to get your new uniform   ☐ yes ☐ no
e) if you still feel nervous about going to secondary school   ☐ yes ☐ no
f) if you also feel excited about going to secondary school   ☐ yes ☐ no
g) if you feel you know what to do if you have a problem at secondary school   ☐ yes ☐ no
h) if you feel ready to move on to secondary school now   ☐ yes ☐ no

5. Open Forum: What positive things were written on my card?

How can I use these qualities in my new school . . .

a) with other students?

b) with adults?

6. Game

a) Did I join in?   ☐ yes ☐ no

b) Did I find an idea of my own?   ☐ yes ☐ no

c) Did I laugh?   ☐ yes ☐ no

7. Round: What did I say?

I offer the people in this group . . .

List some of the things others said:

8. Overall Performance

How did I get on with:

a) being honest about my feelings?   ☐ 1 ☐ 2 ☐ 3 ☐ 4 ☐ 5

b) speaking clearly?   ☐ 1 ☐ 2 ☐ 3 ☐ 4 ☐ 5

c) feeling OK about making mistakes?   ☐ 1 ☐ 2 ☐ 3 ☐ 4 ☐ 5

d) not laughing when other people seem to be making mistakes?   ☐ 1 ☐ 2 ☐ 3 ☐ 4 ☐ 5

e) not feeling embarrassed to speak out?   ☐ 1 ☐ 2 ☐ 3 ☐ 4 ☐ 5

f) giving positive help to other people when they get stuck?   ☐ 1 ☐ 2 ☐ 3 ☐ 4 ☐ 5

9. Did I . . .

a) give a warm signal to anyone?   ☐ yes ☐ no

b) receive a warm signal from anyone?   ☐ yes ☐ no

Teacher comment

Name ⬭⬭⬭⬭⬭⬭⬭⬭⬭⬭⬭⬭⬭⬭ Date ⬭⬭⬭⬭⬭⬭⬭⬭

Student Log   **Transition - Circle Work**

Secondary Session no. 1
Getting to know you

How did I do?   **Self Assessment**

---

1. Rules: How did I get on with . . .

a) respecting others (examples of non-respect: interrupting, put downs, inappropriate laughter or naming someone)?

☐ 1 ☐ 2 ☐ 3 ☐ 4 ☐ 5

b) listening to what everybody else had to say?

☐ 1 ☐ 2 ☐ 3 ☐ 4 ☐ 5

2. Game: Introduce myself and my favourite food

a) Did I introduce myself clearly to the class?   ☐ yes ☐ no

b) Did I introduce my neighbour clearly to the class?   ☐ yes ☐ no

c) Did I stop listening to others when I'd finished my talking?   ☐ yes ☐ no

3. Round: What did I say?

One thing I have enjoyed so far about secondary school is:

⬭⬭⬭⬭⬭⬭⬭⬭⬭⬭⬭⬭⬭⬭⬭⬭⬭⬭⬭⬭⬭⬭⬭⬭⬭⬭⬭⬭⬭⬭

One thing I am concerned/worried about is:

⬭⬭⬭⬭⬭⬭⬭⬭⬭⬭⬭⬭⬭⬭⬭⬭⬭⬭⬭⬭⬭⬭⬭⬭⬭⬭⬭⬭⬭⬭

4. Silent Statement (did I cross the circle?)

a) if you lost your way here today/the first morning   ☐ yes ☐ no

b) if you thought you would but didn't   ☐ yes ☐ no

c) if you're still a little uncomfortable in your school uniform   ☐ yes ☐ no

d) if you're starting to feel comfortable in it   ☐ yes ☐ no

e) if you had a sneaky fashion show with it in front of the mirror during the holidays   ☐ yes ☐ no

f) if you think it's like the land of the giants compared to primary   ☐ yes ☐ no

g) if you like that grown up feeling at secondary school   ☐ yes ☐ no

h) if you're enjoying having all the different lessons to go to   ☐ yes ☐ no

i) if you like having your own planner   ☐ yes ☐ no

j) if you've crossed the circle because somebody else did   ☐ yes ☐ no

k) if you stayed seated because somebody else did   ☐ yes ☐ no

l) if you're beginning to find your way round school   ☐ yes ☐ no

5. Open Forum: What did I say?

a) Would it help if:

b) Something I thought:

6. Game: Dinner

a) Did I join in?   ☐ yes   ☐ no
b) Did I work together with others on an idea?   ☐ yes   ☐ no
c) Did I laugh?   ☐ yes   ☐ no

7. Round: What did I say?
Something positive I have learnt today is:

8. Overall Performance
How did I get on with:

a) being honest about my feelings?   ☐ 1 ☐ 2 ☐ 3 ☐ 4 ☐ 5
b) speaking clearly?   ☐ 1 ☐ 2 ☐ 3 ☐ 4 ☐ 5
c) feeling OK about making mistakes?   ☐ 1 ☐ 2 ☐ 3 ☐ 4 ☐ 5
d) no unkind laughter?   ☐ 1 ☐ 2 ☐ 3 ☐ 4 ☐ 5
e) not feeling embarrassed to speak out?   ☐ 1 ☐ 2 ☐ 3 ☐ 4 ☐ 5
f) looking to see if others need help?   ☐ 1 ☐ 2 ☐ 3 ☐ 4 ☐ 5

9. Did I . . .

a) receive a warm signal from anyone?   ☐ yes   ☐ no
b) give anyone a warm signal?   ☐ yes   ☐ no

Teacher comment

Name ⟨   ⟩   Date ⟨   ⟩

Student Log

Transition - Circle Work

Secondary Session no. 2
Asking for help

How did I do?   **Self Assessment**

---

1. Rules: How did I get on with . . .

a) respecting others (examples of non-respect: interrupting, put downs, inappropriate laughter or naming someone)?

☐ 1 ☐ 2 ☐ 3 ☐ 4 ☐ 5

b) listening to what everybody else had to say?   ☐ 1 ☐ 2 ☐ 3 ☐ 4 ☐ 5

c) respecting group confidentiality over the week?   ☐ 1 ☐ 2 ☐ 3 ☐ 4 ☐ 5

2. Game: Silly Answers

a) Did I ask a question?   ☐ yes ☐ no

b) Did I stand in the middle?   ☐ yes ☐ no

c) Can I control my face muscles when I want to laugh?   ☐ yes ☐ no

3. Round: Pairwork - What did we say?

We might be afraid of asking for help if:

⟨   ⟩

Did I accept other people's fears without criticism?   ☐ yes ☐ no

Is it OK for boys as well as girls to have fears?   ☐ yes ☐ no

4. Silent Statement (did I cross the circle?)

a) if you feel more confident to ask people for help when you know them   ☐ yes ☐ no

b) if you feel less confident to ask for help when you don't know them   ☐ yes ☐ no

c) if you ever feel embarrassed about having got something wrong   ☐ yes ☐ no

d) if you ever want help but feel too stupid/embarrassed to ask   ☐ yes ☐ no

e) if you feel more confident asking for help if you're not the only one   ☐ yes ☐ no

5. Open Forum: Alex doesn't like maths - What did I say?

a) Would it help if:

⟨   ⟩

b) Something I thought:

⟨   ⟩

66

6. Round: What did I say?

How to say what we want politely when we're feeling stressed

When I am upset and angry I:

One way I can stay in control is:

7. Game: Electric Squeeze

a) Did I join in? ☐ yes   ☐ no

b) Did I feel embarrassed about holding hands to begin with? ☐ yes   ☐ no

c) Did I try not to give anything away to the volunteer? ☐ yes   ☐ no

8. Overall Performance

How did I get on with:

a) being honest about my feelings? ☐ 1 ☐ 2 ☐ 3 ☐ 4 ☐ 5

b) speaking clearly? ☐ 1 ☐ 2 ☐ 3 ☐ 4 ☐ 5

c) feeling OK about making mistakes? ☐ 1 ☐ 2 ☐ 3 ☐ 4 ☐ 5

d) not laughing at someone when they're trying to be serious? ☐ 1 ☐ 2 ☐ 3 ☐ 4 ☐ 5

e) not feeling embarrassed to speak out? ☐ 1 ☐ 2 ☐ 3 ☐ 4 ☐ 5

f) offering positive help to others? ☐ 1 ☐ 2 ☐ 3 ☐ 4 ☐ 5

9. Did I . . .

a) give a warm signal? ☐ yes   ☐ no

b) receive a warm signal? ☐ yes   ☐ no

Teacher comment

Name ⬭ Date ⬭

Student Log

Secondary Session no. 3
Dealing with loss

How did I do?   **Self Assessment**

---

1. Rules: How did I get on with . . .

a) respecting others (examples of non-respect: interrupting, put downs, inappropriate laughter or naming someone)?

☐ 1 ☐ 2 ☐ 3 ☐ 4 ☐ 5

b) listening to what everybody else had to say?

☐ 1 ☐ 2 ☐ 3 ☐ 4 ☐ 5

c) respecting group confidentiality over the week?

☐ 1 ☐ 2 ☐ 3 ☐ 4 ☐ 5

2. Game

a) Did I think of a positive adjective to describe myself? ☐ yes ☐ no

b) Did I find out new information about two people? ☐ yes ☐ no

3. Round: In pairs - What did I say?

One thing I miss about my old school is:

⬭

What thing I have gained in my new school is?

⬭

4. Silent Statement (did I cross the circle?)

a) if you can find your way around school now ☐ yes ☐ no

b) if you feel there good things about being at the new school ☐ yes ☐ no

c) if you've talked about your new school to someone at home ☐ yes ☐ no

d) if you felt tired in the first few weeks ☐ yes ☐ no

e) if you feel there are some 'not so good' things about the new school ☐ yes ☐ no

f) if you are missing your old school and teachers ☐ yes ☐ no

g) if you have walked past your old school since you moved ☐ yes ☐ no

h) if you have been back to see your old teacher(s) ☐ yes ☐ no

5. Open Forum: What did I say?

a) Would it help if:

b) Something I could have said but didn't:

6. Game: Rainbow

a) Did I join in?   ☐ yes ☐ no

b) Did I feel OK?   ☐ yes ☐ no

7. Round: What did I say?

Something positive I have learnt today is:

Something else I could have said:

8. Overall Performance

How did I get on with:

a) being honest about my feelings?   ☐ 1 ☐ 2 ☐ 3 ☐ 4 ☐ 5

b) speaking clearly?   ☐ 1 ☐ 2 ☐ 3 ☐ 4 ☐ 5

c) feeling OK about making mistakes?   ☐ 1 ☐ 2 ☐ 3 ☐ 4 ☐ 5

d) feeling OK about other people making mistakes?   ☐ 1 ☐ 2 ☐ 3 ☐ 4 ☐ 5

e) not feeling embarrassed to speak out?   ☐ 1 ☐ 2 ☐ 3 ☐ 4 ☐ 5

9. Did I . . .

a) give a warm signal?   ☐ yes ☐ no

b) receive a warm signal?   ☐ yes ☐ no

Teacher comment

Name		Date	

Student Log

Transition - Circle Work

Secondary Session no. 4
Expectations

How did I do?   **Self Assessment**

---

1. Rules: How did I get on with . . .

a) respecting others (examples of non-respect: interrupting, put downs, inappropriate laughter or naming someone)?

☐ 1 ☐ 2 ☐ 3 ☐ 4 ☐ 5

b) listening to what everybody else had to say?

☐ 1 ☐ 2 ☐ 3 ☐ 4 ☐ 5

c) respecting group confidentiality over the week?

☐ 1 ☐ 2 ☐ 3 ☐ 4 ☐ 5

2. Game: Noise

a) Did I take part?   ☐ yes ☐ no

b) Did I work together and co-operate with a team?   ☐ yes ☐ no

c) Do I think my team worked imaginatively?   ☐ yes ☐ no

3. Round: What did I say?

Now I'm in secondary school I feel people expect me to:

What else could I have said?

4. Silent Statement (did I cross the circle?)

a) if you've had an argument with an adult in the morning   ☐ yes ☐ no

b) if you're expected to be more responsible now you're at secondary school   ☐ yes ☐ no

c) if what you want and what adults want for you are sometimes different   ☐ yes ☐ no

d) if you feel you're sometimes still treated too much like a child   ☐ yes ☐ no

e) if you sometimes behave like an adult   ☐ yes ☐ no

f) if you sometimes behave like a child (be honest!)   ☐ yes ☐ no

g) if you think you're expected to remember a lot now you're at secondary school ☐ yes ☐ no

h) if you get more freedom now you're at secondary school   ☐ yes ☐ no

l) if you wish you were given more freedom   ☐ yes ☐ no

j) if you're expected to fit more things into your life now you're secondary   ☐ yes ☐ no

k) if you've found yourself running out of time a lot more than before   ☐ yes ☐ no

l) if you're expected to help round the house more as you get older   ☐ yes ☐ no

m) if you feel you're expected to know more than you do   ☐ yes ☐ no

5. Open Forum: Alex feels people are expecting too much - What did I say?

a) Would it help if:

b) Something I could have said but didn't:

6. Game: I love you honey

a) Did I join in? ☐ yes ☐ no

b) Did I use good eye contact? ☐ yes ☐ no

c) Did I use positive body language? ☐ yes ☐ no

7. Round: What did I say?

Something positive that I expect from myself while at secondary school is:

Something else I could have said:

8. Overall Performance

How did I get on with:

a) being honest about my feelings? ☐ 1 ☐ 2 ☐ 3 ☐ 4 ☐ 5

b) speaking clearly? ☐ 1 ☐ 2 ☐ 3 ☐ 4 ☐ 5

c) feeling OK about making mistakes? ☐ 1 ☐ 2 ☐ 3 ☐ 4 ☐ 5

d) feeling OK about what I've said? ☐ 1 ☐ 2 ☐ 3 ☐ 4 ☐ 5

e) not feeling embarrassed to speak out? ☐ 1 ☐ 2 ☐ 3 ☐ 4 ☐ 5

f) giving positive help to other people when they get stuck? ☐ 1 ☐ 2 ☐ 3 ☐ 4 ☐ 5

9. Did I . . .

a) give a warm signal to someone I've not given one to before? ☐ yes ☐ no

b) receive a warm signal from someone I've not had one from before? ☐ yes ☐ no

Teacher comment

Student Log

Transition - Circle Work

Secondary Session no. 5
Friendships

How did I do?   Self Assessment

1. Rules: How did I get on with . . .

a) respecting others (examples of non-respect: interrupting, put downs, inappropriate laughter or naming someone)?

◻ 1 ◻ 2 ◻ 3 ◻ 4 ◻ 5

b) listening to what everybody else had to say?

◻ 1 ◻ 2 ◻ 3 ◻ 4 ◻ 5

c) respecting group confidentiality over the week?

◻ 1 ◻ 2 ◻ 3 ◻ 4 ◻ 5

2. Game: Elephant, palm tree and aeroplane

a) Did I take part?   ◻ yes ◻ no
b) Did I work together and co-operate with groups of three?   ◻ yes ◻ no
c) Did I concentrate so I didn't miss my turn?   ◻ yes ◻ no

3. Round: What did I say? When friendships go wrong I feel . . .

Write five words that other people said too:

⟨ ⟩

4. Silent Statement (did I cross the circle?)

a) if you came from primary school with friends   ◻ yes ◻ no
b) if you knew someone already at the secondary school   ◻ yes ◻ no
c) if you have already made some new friends   ◻ yes ◻ no
d) if you have noticed your old friends making new friends   ◻ yes ◻ no
e) if there are friends in this class whom you would like to be able to trust   ◻ yes ◻ no
f) if you have ever gone around in a crowd   ◻ yes ◻ no
g) if you ever had someone you have thought of as a best friend   ◻ yes ◻ no
h) if you ever felt let down and hurt by a friend   ◻ yes ◻ no
i) if a friend has ever felt you had let them down   ◻ yes ◻ no
j) if you forgive people easily   ◻ yes ◻ no
k) if someone has ever forgiven you   ◻ yes ◻ no
l) if you think it's better to sort arguments out rather than let them carry on   ◻ yes ◻ no
m) if you've ever felt left out   ◻ yes ◻ no
n) if you think it possible to have a lot of good friends   ◻ yes ◻ no

5. Open Forum: Alex feels left out - What did I say?

a) Would it help if:

b) Any other thoughts:

6. Game

a) Did I join in?	☐ yes ☐ no
b) Did I work well with my partner?	☐ yes ☐ no

7. Round: What did I say?

When I'm a good friend I:

Something else I could have said:

8. Overall Performance

How did I get on with:

a) being honest about my feelings?	☐ 1 ☐ 2 ☐ 3 ☐ 4 ☐ 5
b) speaking clearly?	☐ 1 ☐ 2 ☐ 3 ☐ 4 ☐ 5
c) feeling OK about making mistakes?	☐ 1 ☐ 2 ☐ 3 ☐ 4 ☐ 5
d) feeling OK about what I've said?	☐ 1 ☐ 2 ☐ 3 ☐ 4 ☐ 5
e) not feeling embarrassed to speak out?	☐ 1 ☐ 2 ☐ 3 ☐ 4 ☐ 5
f) giving positive help to other people when they get stuck?	☐ 1 ☐ 2 ☐ 3 ☐ 4 ☐ 5

9. Did I . . .

a) give a warm signal to someone I've not given one to before?	☐ yes ☐ no
b) receive a warm signal from someone I've not had one from before?	☐ yes ☐ no

Teacher comment

Name

Date

Student Log

Transition - Circle Work

Secondary Session no. 6
How am I doing so far?

How did I do?   **Self Assessment**

---

1. Rules: How did I get on with . . .

a) respecting others (examples of non-respect: interrupting, put downs, inappropriate laughter or naming someone)?

☐ 1 ☐ 2 ☐ 3 ☐ 4 ☐ 5

b) listening to what everybody else had to say?

☐ 1 ☐ 2 ☐ 3 ☐ 4 ☐ 5

c) respecting group confidentiality over the week?

☐ 1 ☐ 2 ☐ 3 ☐ 4 ☐ 5

2. Game

a) Did I co-operate with others?   ☐ yes ☐ no
b) Did I help others?   ☐ yes ☐ no
c) Did I feel helped by others?   ☐ yes ☐ no

3. Round: What did I say?

Two things we have found difficult:

Did I want to say anything else?

What?

4. Silent Statement (did I cross the circle?)

a) if you have found it hard getting up earlier in the morning   ☐ yes ☐ no
b) if you have got used to getting up earlier now   ☐ yes ☐ no
c) if you have found it hard getting used to all the different teachers   ☐ yes ☐ no
d) if you feel you're getting used to all the different teachers   ☐ yes ☐ no
e) if you're used to the new routines of secondary school   ☐ yes ☐ no
f) if you think you can remember most of your school timetable now   ☐ yes ☐ no
g) if you are using your planner every day   ☐ yes ☐ no
h) if you are mostly remembering to bring the things you need   ☐ yes ☐ no
i) if you are pleased with the new friends you are making   ☐ yes ☐ no
j) if you are enjoying most of your lessons   ☐ yes ☐ no
k) if you feel you're a different person now than before the summer holidays ☐ yes ☐ no
l) if you feel to have learnt a lot about 'life' since primary school   ☐ yes ☐ no

5. Open Forum: Star students - What did my stars say?

a) Our two stars were:

b) Something I could have chosen but didn't:

6. Game
a) Did I join in? ☐ yes ☐ no
b) Did I work together on an idea? ☐ yes ☐ no

7. Round: What did I say?
Our team has done well because:

8. Overall Performance
How did I get on with:

a) being honest about my feelings? ☐ 1 ☐ 2 ☐ 3 ☐ 4 ☐ 5

b) speaking clearly? ☐ 1 ☐ 2 ☐ 3 ☐ 4 ☐ 5

c) feeling OK about making mistakes? ☐ 1 ☐ 2 ☐ 3 ☐ 4 ☐ 5

d) not laughing when other people seem to be making mistakes? ☐ 1 ☐ 2 ☐ 3 ☐ 4 ☐ 5

e) not feeling embarrassed to speak out? ☐ 1 ☐ 2 ☐ 3 ☐ 4 ☐ 5

f) giving positive help to other people when they get stuck? ☐ 1 ☐ 2 ☐ 3 ☐ 4 ☐ 5

9. Did I . . .
a) give a warm signal to anyone? ☐ yes ☐ no
b) receive a warm signal from anyone? ☐ yes ☐ no

Teacher comment

75

Parent/Student Taster Day

Alex's day at Secondary School

Questions to ask at first in order to get a feel for who Alex is (try to keep Alex as gender-less as possible):

- What is Alex's favourite TV programme?
- What are Alex's favourite sweets?
- What is Alex's favourite pop group?
- What does Alex do on a Saturday?
- What was the last item of clothing that Alex bought?
- It's Alex's birthday next month. What does Alex want?

> **Ask group members to move to one side of the room for negative feelings and the other for positive feelings. The asterisks denote moments when members will decide which side to be on.**

Alex comes home from school and chills out watching a video of .... *whilst tucking into .... *Alex looks back on the day and remembers the credit the teacher gave for the good work Alex did in maths*. Alex shows the credit in the planner to Dad. Dad is really pleased too and praises Alex*.

Alex remembers that the teacher talked about being organised* and doing homework as soon as you get home* and continues to watch TV whilst beginning the story that Mrs Clark asked the class to write for homework*. [Teacher needs to point out that quality of homework is much better when done away from distractions like the TV - it gets finished quicker and is less stressful for parents too. If space is a problem then a bed is better than nothing]

Suddenly the phone rings and Alex runs to answer it. Alex's best friend asks Alex to go skateboarding at the new skateboard park*. Alex thinks about the homework and thinks 'I can do it in registration time tomorrow,' grabs a coat and goes out*.

Baby brother meanwhile rather likes the look of Alex's homework and begins to draw with Alex's felt tips*. Alex returns to find beautiful patterns and squiggles all over the homework. Alex shouts at Dad, 'Why didn't you stop him!'* Dad stays calm at first, sympathising* until he realises that Alex had not finished the homework. He gets angry too* and says 'If it was important, why didn't you finish the homework and put it away in a safe place? You shouldn't have gone out without finishing it, and you know what babies are like. Anyway if you hadn't sat in front of the TV you would have finished it in time to go out.'* A big argument follows* and then Alex gets sent to bed.

Alex goes to bed in tears* but through the tiredness remembers to pack the school bag ready for tomorrow*. Alex is too tired to think carefully though, and forgets to pack the PE kit*. Dad de-stresses himself with a soak in the bath.

Ten minutes before the alarm goes off, Alex awakes* and decides to go for a bath *.........but then on second thoughts decides that deodorant is just as effective.* Alex gets dressed and sniffs - oh oh, the shirt's a bit smelly*. Never mind, another quick spray of deodorant all over should do it*.

Alex goes downstairs and remembers the importance of having breakfast before school - doesn't really feel hungry but has a slice of toast and glass of milk*. By the back door, the black shoes belonging to Alex look incredibly clean and Alex realises that Dad must have cleaned them*. Pleased, Alex goes to Dad to thank him*. Dad says that he's going to clean them for Alex for the next three weeks until Alex settles into school some more. Alex feels good about that*.

Outside the gate, Alex's friend Jo says, 'Can't wait for PE today. I really like Miss Smith.' Oh no, Alex thinks, 'my PE kit!'* Alex rushes back in. 'Dad, did you wash my PE kit?' Dad replies, 'Alex, did you ask me to wash it?' Alex finds the PE kit crumpled in a corner of the bedroom*. 'I can't wear this,' Alex says. 'You'll have to,' says Dad. 'You don't have a spare kit. You'll have to hurry or else you'll be late.'

Jo and Alex make it to school with a few minutes to spare*. A moment later, a teacher pulls them up for running along the corridor*. They get to their classroom on time and Alex shows the teacher the planner which Alex has remembered to ask Dad to sign.*

PSHE Homework

Name (....) *Date* (...............................)

My poster of when I behaved positively towards someone (was good to someone)

[blank box]

Tick the quality behaviours which were shown to you (it might be more than one):
☐ kindness   ☐ love   ☐ encouragement   ☐ praise   ☐ patience   ☐ caring
☐ trust   ☐ co-operation   ☐ support   ☐ listening   ☐ taking the time
☐ understanding   ☐ knowing when to give you space   ☐ sensitive
☐ forgiving   ☐ sharing   ☐ protective

Add any others

[blank box]

Find someone who . . .

- is going to visit their secondary school

> name:

- knows one thing they could do if they were being teased

> name:

- would go up in a friendly way if they saw someone looking a bit lonely / scared

> name:

- thinks it's OK to ask for help if you get stuck on something

> name:

- can think of three changes that might happen as a consequence of going to secondary school

> name:

- can think of one thing they are looking forward to

> name:

- has had a dream about going to secondary school

> name:

- can think of one thing they are not looking forward to

> name:

- might miss their friends

> name:

- is looking forward to making new friends

> name:

- is worried about the homework they might receive

> name:

Friendship Bingo

Find someone who . . .

- **has spoken to someone new today**

  name:

- **likes baked beans**

  name:

- **would help someone if they were lost**

  name:

- **watches 'Friends' on TV**

  name:

- **thought they would get lost**

  name:

- **is from a different school from yourself**

  name:

- **likes something that you like**

  name:

- **is the eldest child at home**

  name:

- **reads Goosebumps books**

  name:

- **would help someone if they were being bullied**

  name:

appendix 8

Scenarios for use in Open Forum

(Characters can be girl or boy)

1. I'm new and don't really know many people at this school - none of them are in my class. Trouble is I'm shy and not very good at making friends and I'm not so good at all the things they seem to be good at so I feel a bit useless. Nobody seems to notice me, they're all so wrapped up with their own friends. I really miss my old school and friends and teachers - everybody knew me. It feels lonely and I don't have much protection. Somebody had a go at me in the playground the other day and I'm frightened it will happen again.

2. I keep getting into arguments with my Mum and Dad. Ever since I started the new school, they've been on at me to remember this, to do that, to stop doing this, to do my homework, to help with the housework, to tidy my bedroom. I can't seem to move without them criticising me. I'm fed up and feel like running away sometimes. I lost my new jacket the other day and they went ballistic shouting at me. It was in the morning just before I left for school - I didn't dare tell them I'd lost it at school but they found out. I was in tears when I left home. I just keep getting into arguments with them.

3. I feel really down. My friend and I are from the same primary school and we moved up to secondary school together. We always used to be good mates but now somebody else has started hanging around - someone who lives near my friend. They went out together last night without me and were talking about it all day today and I feel really mad and upset that I wasn't invited. Also I don't know what this new friend thinks of me - I get the feeling I'm not wanted. I feel really hurt and let down.

4. Mornings are just a complete nightmare for me. I'm so tired I can't get up and then when I do it's just mad at our house. I can't get in the bathroom because my sister is in the bathroom for ages. I get told off for taking ages getting dressed. I usually end up going without breakfast because I'm too late. I'm always forgetting my planner. I showed it to my Mum once and then I keep forgetting to put it in my bag.

5. I'm worried about going to PE because I'll have to get changed in front of others and I'm worried that people will take the mickey out of the way I look. I worry myself till I feel sick about it. It starts the night before when I usually cry and can't get to sleep. I can't help the way I am and I feel really jealous of those people who aren't fat. They don't have to worry about this. I've had it before at primary school. Not everybody's like that - some people care. They're the really brave ones. I don't know why they don't tease me. I suppose they must respect me and try to understand how it must feel. It helps me if people don't tease me, though that doesn't stop the bullies from calling me names.

Cut Out Stars

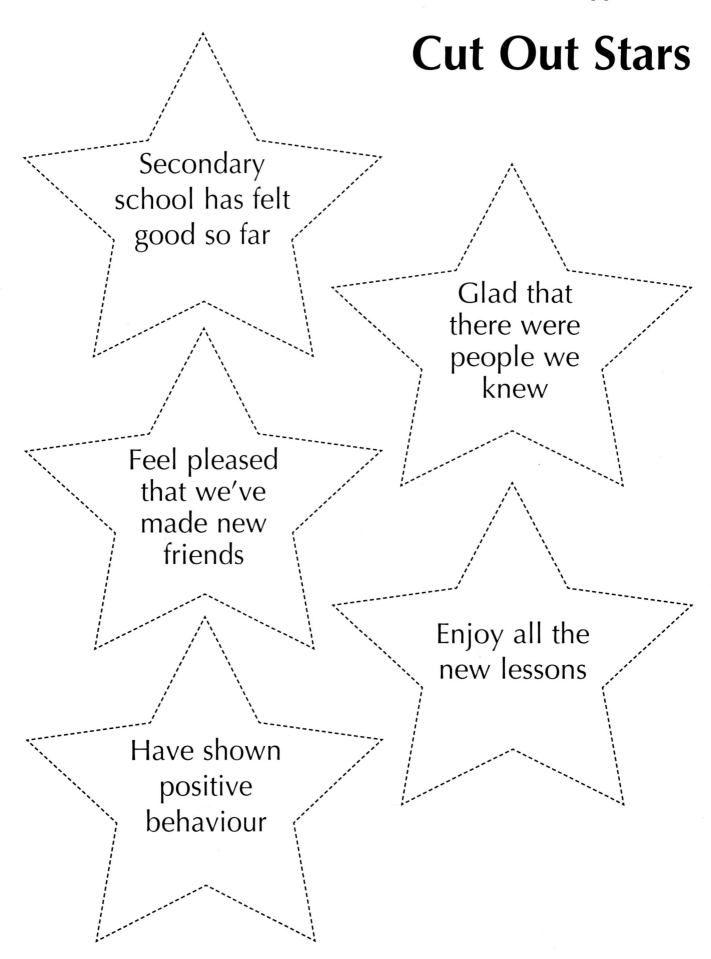

Secondary school has felt good so far

Glad that there were people we knew

Feel pleased that we've made new friends

Enjoy all the new lessons

Have shown positive behaviour

Cut Out Stars

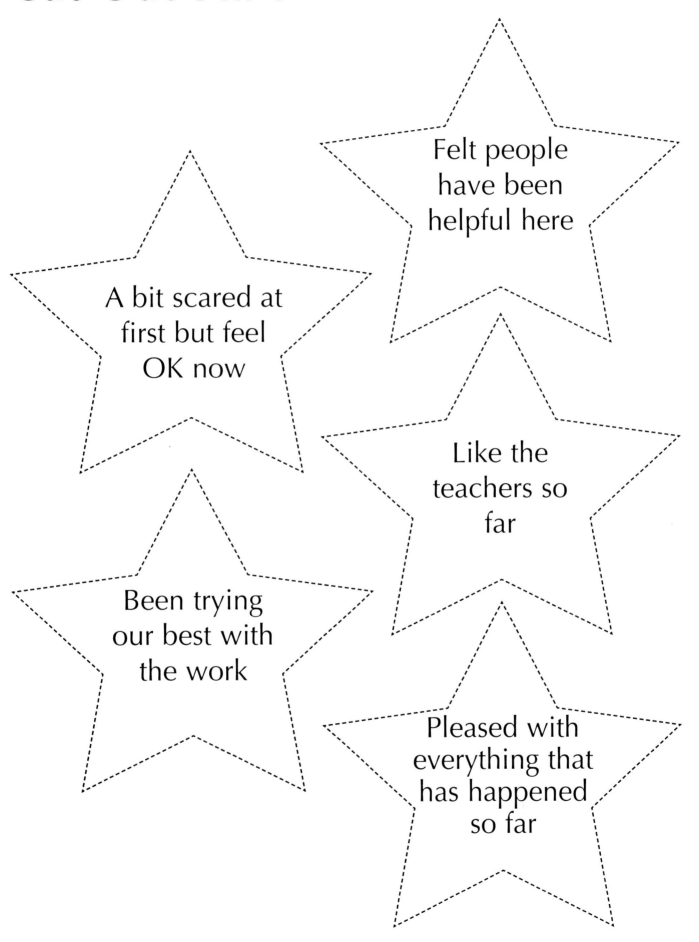

Felt people have been helpful here

A bit scared at first but feel OK now

Like the teachers so far

Been trying our best with the work

Pleased with everything that has happened so far

Cut Out Stars

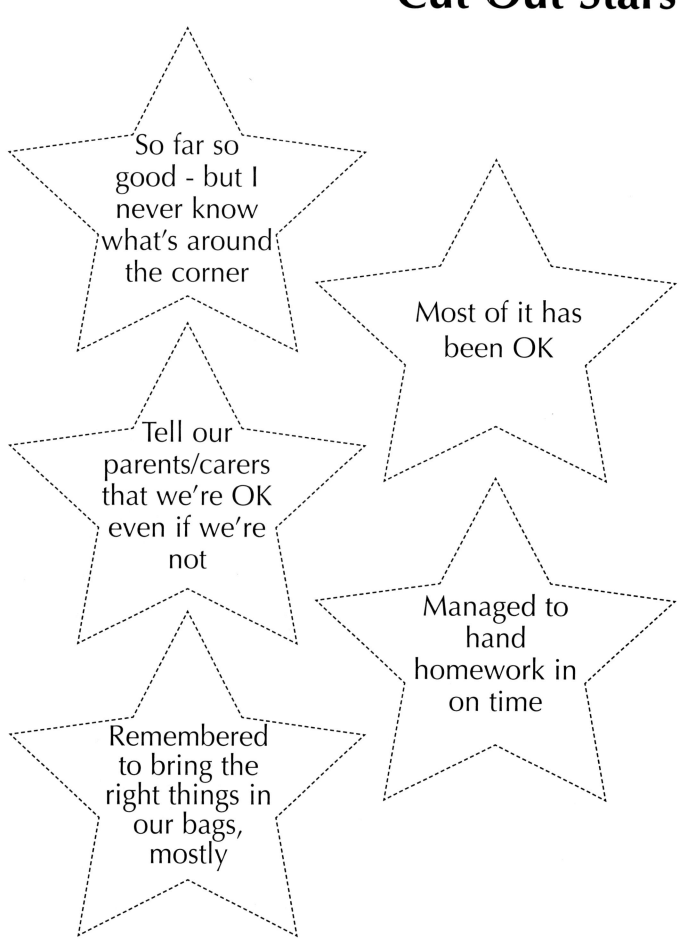

So far so good - but I never know what's around the corner

Most of it has been OK

Tell our parents/carers that we're OK even if we're not

Managed to hand homework in on time

Remembered to bring the right things in our bags, mostly

Cut Out Stars

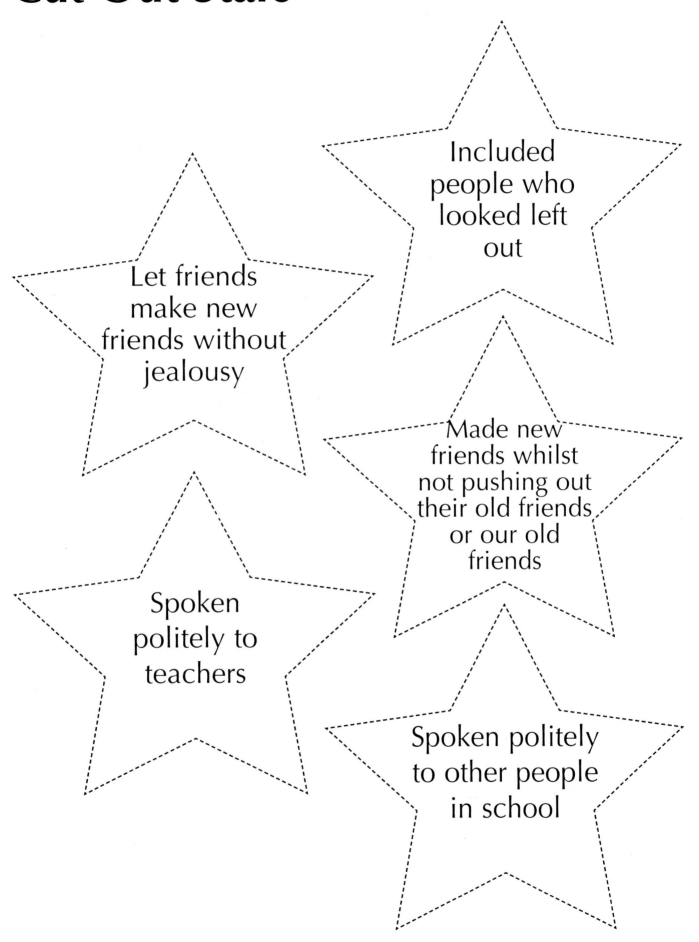

Included people who looked left out

Let friends make new friends without jealousy

Made new friends whilst not pushing out their old friends or our old friends

Spoken politely to teachers

Spoken politely to other people in school

Cut Out Stars

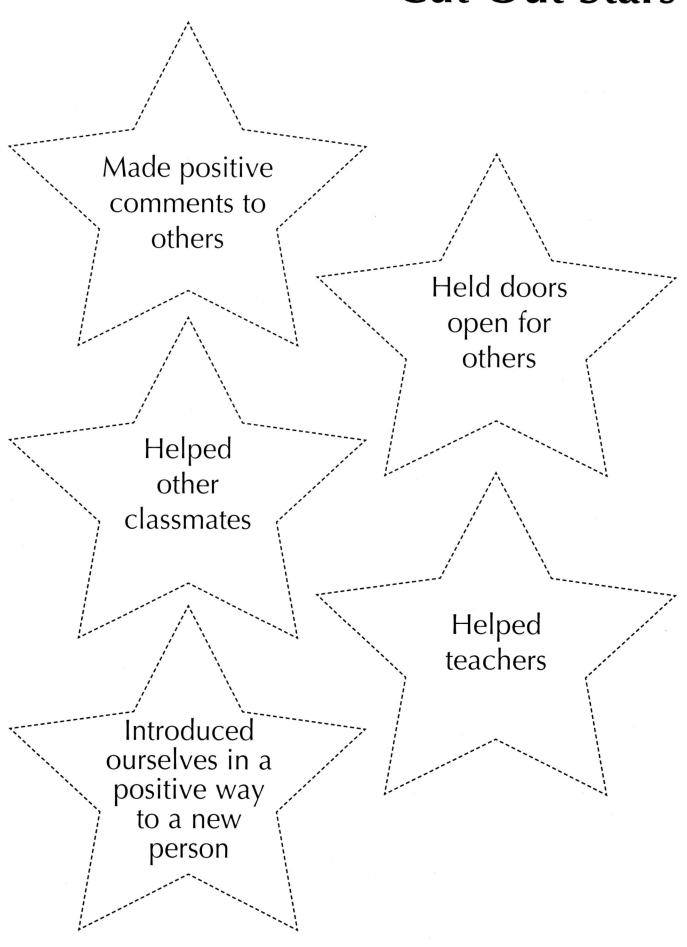

Made positive comments to others

Held doors open for others

Helped other classmates

Helped teachers

Introduced ourselves in a positive way to a new person

Cut Out Stars

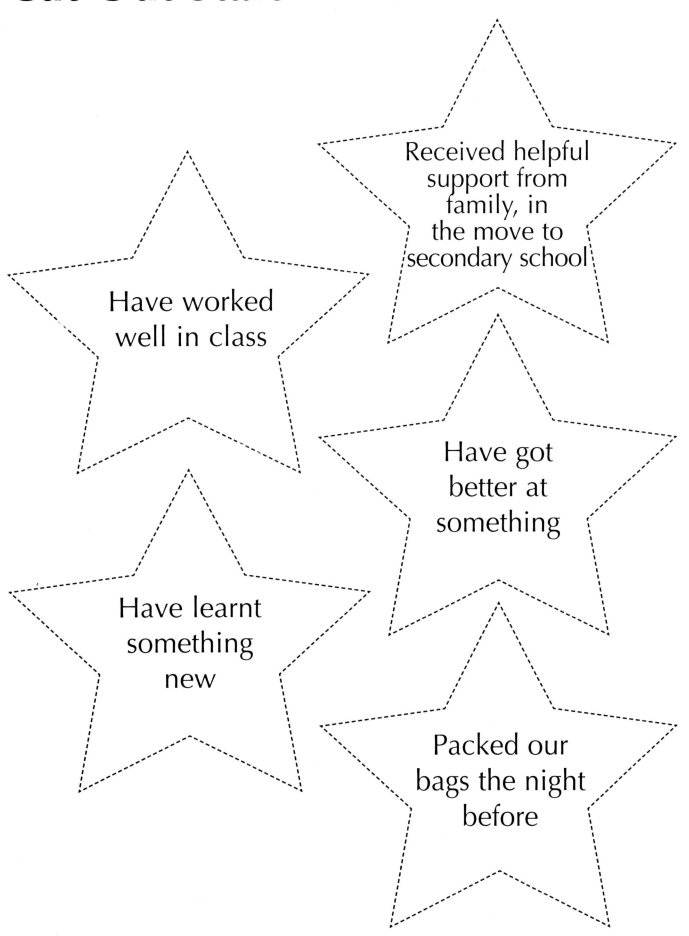

Received helpful
support from
family, in
the move to
secondary school

Have worked
well in class

Have got
better at
something

Have learnt
something
new

Packed our
bags the night
before

Cut Out Stars

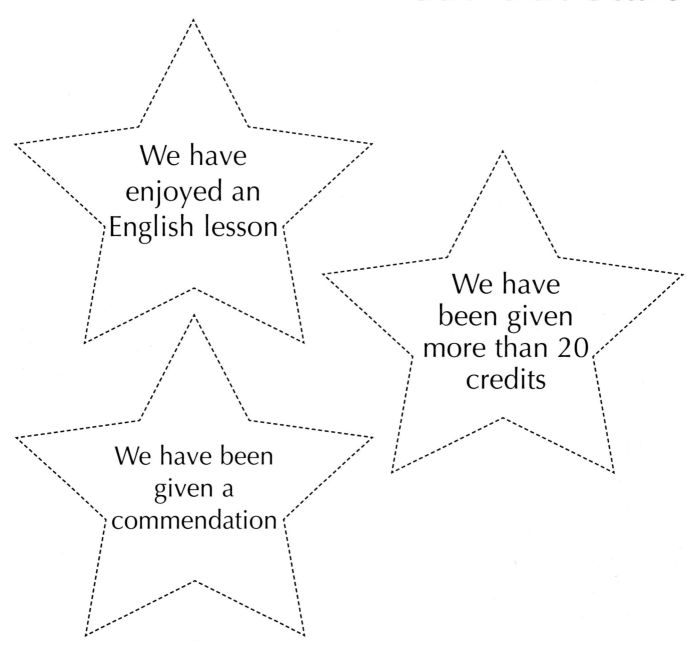

We have enjoyed an English lesson

We have been given more than 20 credits

We have been given a commendation

Celebration Cards

Make these using the photo of the whole class that you took in Lesson 1, and add a message such as 'Welcome Saira, well done for successfully completing the transition to Blenfield High School course. Thank you for all your thoughtful contributions. We look forward to more of these.'

appendix 10

Training and resources available from Jenny Mosley Consultancies and Positive Press

Training Opportunities

Jenny Mosley Consultancies are able to offer a wide range of courses, all encompassed within the framework of her Whole School Quality Circle Time Model. We have a small team of highly experienced consultants available to meet the specific requirements of individual schools.

Some of the courses we offer:

Releasing excellence through Quality Circle Time: an introduction (for primary and secondary schools). Like all our courses, this can be run as a closure (INSET) day or within a working school day. During a closure day all teaching and ancillary staff are invited to focus on the Quality Circle Time Model and its possibilities for creating a shared vision. On a working school day the consultant will demonstrate Quality Circle Time meetings with whole classes of children with an alternating range of staff observing. A specific circle session is held for lunchtime supervisors and the day will conclude with debriefing and action planning. The most effective package is to book these (on consecutive days) plus a follow up review day.

If your school is already using Circle Time and is ready to review your progress and move on, then you will find our in-depth modules really useful. Or perhaps you feel that colleagues have lost their first burst of Quality Circle Time enthusiasm, and need a refresher. Courses for you include:

Developing the Quality Circle Time Model
Happier Lunchtimes
Assessing Effectiveness of Self-Esteem, Anti-bullying and Positive Behaviour Policies
Peer Mediation
Meeting PSHE and Citizenship Requirements through Quality Circle Time
Re-energising Quality Circle Time
Children Beyond - Play therapy as a way forward
Involving Parents and Governors in Quality Circle Time

Quality Circle Time mentoring is also available, as are courses in staff development and support covering areas such as team-building, stress management, developing your own self-esteem, boosting your energy and basic counselling skills.

Accredited, specialist trainers only!

Our research and experience have revealed that the Whole School Quality Circle Time Model can become diluted or vulnerable when people who have never attended one of our in-depth courses themselves give training based on our model. Jenny Mosley holds five-day accredited 'Train the Trainers' courses nationally and then awards accompanying certificates. A full list of accredited trainers is available.

For details of all the above, contact the Project Manager by any of the means listed at the end of this section.

Books and other resources

Turn Your School Round by Jenny Mosley (LDA)
Best-selling management manual giving a clear picture of the Quality Circle Time approach, emphasising the need for it to be a whole school policy and including guidelines and practical examples for a range of situations.

Quality Circle Time in the Primary Classroom by Jenny Mosley (LDA)
Invaluable guide to getting started and building strategies to promote self-esteem and positive behaviour, for teachers wishing to put the Whole School Quality Circle Time model into their classrooms, with hundreds of ideas and lesson plans.

More Quality Circle Time by Jenny Mosley (LDA)
Sequel to the above enabling you to evaluate and enhance your current Circle Time practice, raising it to even more exciting and creative levels.

Photocopiable Materials for use with the Jenny Mosley Circle Time Model by Jenny Mosley (Positive Press)
Make life easier with a wealth of charts, target sheets, achievement ladders, awards, congratulations cards, invitations and much more, including tips to help you quickly put them to good use.

Important Issues Relating to the Promotion of Positive Behaviour and Self-Esteem in Secondary Schools by Jenny Mosley (Positive Press)
90-page booklet introducing the model and explaining its rationale and use at this level, with more advanced exercises and ideas on how to improve communication skills, self-esteem, effective sanctions and incentives, stress awareness and more.

Quality Circle Time in the Secondary School by Jenny Mosley and Marilyn Tew (David Fulton Publishers)
Showing it's never too late to introduce circle time, this book offers themed activities, practical strategies and case studies. Building 'emotional literacy' and respectful assertiveness through circle time will complement your behaviour management and anti-bullying policies.

Circle Time (Positive Press)
User-friendly booklet built around Jenny Mosley's whole school approach, with practical lesson plans for KS1 and KS2 based on an original project in Belfast and now updated.

The Circle Book by Jenny Mosley (Positive Press)
A booklet of feedback and comments (by children and adults) originally compiled in response to the Elton Report (1989) and building on research study results. Updated with more ideas for activities.

Working Towards a Whole School Policy on Self-Esteem and Positive Behaviour by Jenny Mosley (Positive Press)
A booklet of guidelines for operating an effective policy involving teachers, MDSAs, parents, governors and children.

All Round Success by Jenny Mosley (Wiltshire County Council)
Simply set-out practical ideas and games for circle time, tried and tested in a year-long project with primary teachers.

Coming Round Again by Jenny Mosley (Wiltshire County Council)

Follows on from the above, pulling together a range of fun activities that provide excellent learning opportunities for PSHE and citizenship themes. Explains the rationale behind Circle Time and includes problem-solving ideas.

Guidelines for Primary Midday Supervisors by Jenny Mosley (Wiltshire County Council)

A friendly self-help booklet for lunchtime supervisors to use in developing skills in their role as positive models for the children, supporting your school in the creation of secure and happy playtimes.

Create Happier Lunchtimes by Jenny Mosley (Wiltshire County Council)

Sequel to the above, reminding lunchtime supervisors of the importance of their role, offering extra ideas and both indoor and outdoor games.

Assemblies to Teach Golden Rules by Margaret Goldthorpe and Lucy Nutt (LDA)

Ideal if your assemblies could use more 'pep'! Scripts and ideas for creative, fun presentations themed on the moral values behind Golden Rules, based on positive reward for good behaviour rather than punishment for negative actions.

Effective IEPs Through Circle Time by Margaret Goldthorpe (LDA)

Practical solutions to writing Individual Education Plans for children with emotional and behavioural difficulties. Case studies and photocopiable charts offer lots of practical, down to earth ideas.

Poems for Circle Time and Literacy Hour by Margaret Goldthorpe (LDA)

A much loved book by one of Jenny's senior consultants. Poems of simplicity and fun introduce children in a relaxed way to serious issues such as bullying and can then provide the theme for circle time.

Training video: Quality Circle Time in Action (LDA)

Introduced and performed by Jenny Mosley and ideal for staff training, this video demonstrates the model in use with unrehearsed KS1 and KS2 children. The phases and their rationale are explained by Jenny using many of the resources listed here for sale. Handbook included.

Jenny Mosley's Self-Esteem Builders Set

Set of colourful high-quality resources to get your school quickly started with Quality Circle Time. Contains motivational stickers for congratulating children on moral values and circle time skills; class target sheets with reusable stickers to mark progress in positive behaviour; reward certificates for achievements; responsibility badges for boosting children's self-esteem through special tasks; and a golden rules poster set (see below). Items also available separately.

Golden Rules Poster Set

Displaying the do's and don'ts of positive behaviour that lie at the heart of Quality Circle Time, in a choice of size and material suitable for indoors or out.

Jenny Mosley's Quality Circle Time Kitbag

Costume and treasures to inspire creative circle times: contains 'magic' cloak, blindfold, hand-painted egg (for use as talking object), South American rainstick, small teddy bear, two hand puppets and 'treasure chest', together with cassette tape and booklet of lesson ideas. Rainstick, eggs and puppets also available separately.

Playground Friends Cap and Hats

Brightly coloured incentives to support your whole school lunchtime policy, which advocates choosing pupil helpers to befriend marginalised or bewildered children. A 'badge of office' to be worn with pride. Playground Stops for children seeking help also available.

101 Games for Social Skills by Jenny Mosley & Helen Sonnet (LDA)

Creative and dynamic games that will help develop positive relationships and the skills of healthy interactions. Some tried and tested and some brand new, but all enormous fun.

Clapping Games by Jenny Mosley & Helen Sonnet (Positive Press Ltd)

A collection that includes old favourites together with brand new games in a superb, easy-to-use A3 size to share with the whole class. The fascinating illustrations by Mark Cripps will enchant any child.

All Year Round by Jenny Mosley & Georgia Thorp (LDA)

Here is a manual packed with all you will ever need for creating happier lunchtimes. Look no further for fully tested ideas covering every crucial aspect, from zoning the playground and training Playground Friends to raising the morale of midday supervisors and bringing in the outside community.

101 Games for Self-Esteem by Jenny Mosley & Helen Sonnet (LDA)

A clearly set out book of games which focus on self-affirmation, team building, art, music, drama, verbal and written themes, physical activity and relaxation. Creating a positive atmosphere, these activities relate to the key skills and enable children to develop their self-confidence whilst having fun.

Further titles in preparation:

Golden Moments for Busy Teachers (Positive Press)

The Golden Rules Series - stories to illustrate each of the golden rules. Large format books with accompanying finger puppets. (Positive Press Ltd)

Skipping Games (Positive Press Ltd)

We also have books on Quality Circle Time for the Early Years, and on self-esteem and assertiveness for adults including those with learning difficulties ... ask for details.

For further details and to order contact:

Jenny Mosley Consultancies / Positive Press Ltd

Tel. 01225 767157 *(training)*   Tel. 01225 719204 *(books and resources)*

Fax. 01225 755631

E-mail circletime@jennymosley.demon.co.uk

28A Gloucester Road
Trowbridge
Wiltshire
BA14 0AA

Website: www.circle-time.co.uk